Words
to
See By

Words
to
See By

by Miriam F. Bolduan

FORTRESS PRESS
Philadelphia

Contents

Verbal Portrait

Reluctant to grow up,
One longs for the simple speech of childhood,
Forgetting the multiple connotations
Of fear and joy, of hate and pride, of love and envy
That surround, for the baby, his one word:
Mine.

Maturation is a continuous battle
Against the temptation to simplify;
A continuous building of the vocabulary
Needed to erect tight shelters, secret passages, and
    mighty fortresses;
A continuous camouflaging of thought or emotion
That might otherwise reveal one's hidden mastery.

Youth is naïve to expect direct speech
When safety lies in duplicity.

Yet, I speak as a fool,
Lapsing into childish openness,
Into frank declarations of love,
Into boastings in weaknesses,
In the impudent belief that among the multitudes
Is one who will recognize, in every letter of mine,
The mark; for it is the way I write.

A Word to the Reader

On Learning
the Language

To teach Americans a second language is, in many parts of the country at least, difficult because the students have little opportunity to hear anything but contemporary American English spoken naturally, and even less opportunity to speak anything else themselves. When I was a very young child, I occasionally heard foreign-born Americans speak their various native languages. Though no great attempt was made to teach these to me, I learned a few rhymes and phrases, and I saw about me symbols and mottoes in the one particular language which became, by its daily or weekly presence, most a part of me. Some thirty years later, I found myself in the country where that language is the mother tongue. I was, at last, at home.

To teach young city dwellers "nature study" isn't easy either—at least not any easier than to teach small-town dwellers the wonders of the Boston public transit system. Yet, when I moved to an area where those picture-book birds of which I had been taught as a child truly lived and sang, I was equally "at home." The same thing happens whether one studies history or languages, science or art. Suddenly, upon contact with the real thing in its native setting, one is at home.

Such an experience, repeated in so many varieties, is not without ultimate significance.

As long as I can remember, I have heard words which are a part of the language of still another country; one day I shall find myself there, and I shall be at home. In the meantime, I look for and listen for others who know the language; I look for and listen for, in the writing and speech of this country, passwords which indicate a knowledge of the other country. In fact, I believe it could be said of certain people I have known that their whole purpose in living was to keep this second language alive—to discover and use its vocabulary themselves and to pass it on from one generation to another.

To enlarge one's vocabulary in such a new language, one must constantly, in daily experience, test new words. One may also learn from one's trusted friends, whose words correspond to experience, or one may learn from others who have been trustworthy in the past and who are therefore reliable witnesses. The best way to enlarge the word treasury suddenly, though, is to discover the system which is at the base of the knowledge of everything this language can express.

The system is extremely simple: all of nature, all
of man, and all of God exist in patterns. Therefore,
were I to describe a given trait in man, I should
expect to find a parallel trait in both God and nature.
Should I describe a system of law, I should expect to
find a comparable system in all three situations: a
law of nature, a law of man (single and communal),
and a law of God. Should I find, in regard to human
life, families, I should expect to find families in
nature, and, within the nature of God himself, a
comparable "family."

The system is simple. The basic vocabulary is
simple enough. But for an adult, in love with the
wonder of life, the variations throughout all of time
and space become infinitely complex.

Words
to
See By

Passwords

The words we speak serve two functions: to divide and to unite. This is most certainly true. There are problems which I cannot by my own reason or strength overcome; there are societies which I cannot with my own basic nature enter; but as soon as I have been taught the proper words, as soon as I have learned the necessary vocabulary, the obstacles are overcome, and I may enter the "paradise" of those in the know. The same words which formerly divided strangers now serve to unite friends.

A single password may admit me to fellowship with my neighbor, or a whole new vocabulary may be necessary. If I wish to join the American Chemical Society, I must have studied its particular vocabulary; if I wish to join the National Education Association, I must know another set of words. Should I wish to join a professional society in another country, the problem multiplies, for then I must not only learn the suitable technical language, but also translate it into a foreign language. On the other hand, to enter the kingdom of heaven I need know essentially one word: *Father*.

But I must know what that one word means.

In the first place, the word *Father*, for all the one-ness of God, is not a word which stands alone. A dictionary may define *father* as the male parent, but such a definition itself implies the existence of a child, which further implies the existence of a mother. One word may be the password to eternal life, to acceptance as a child of God as well as to the secrets of life on earth; but that one word is in itself a whole library of ideas out of which to build a complete life.

This one word, *Father*, opens the door to the whole history of mankind. The recognition of a basic pattern throughout creation makes possible, for the busy mother of small children, for the involved father at his workbench, as well as for the philosopher in his book-lined office, the understanding of the most profound truths of all eternity.

Unless, of course, out of the one word are developed specialized vocabularies with the conscious intention to divide. The educator, the internist, and the ballet dancer may speak quite different languages even though they all speak English, and their vocabularies are more likely to divide than to unite them. Yet, as human beings, they may share the common vocabulary of the children of One Father.

Did the building of the Tower of Babel itself bring about the confusion of languages among men? Did this confusion arise when men separated themselves into diggers, water carriers, farmers, brickmakers, architects, irrigation engineers, bricklayers, and cooks for the project? Did confusion arise when the vocabularies of men ceased to be the unifying language of the family and became instead the divisive language of specialization?

Today, as artists and physicians and lawyers and teachers, as stenographers and students and senators and lobbyists, we speak languages which divide. The current "gaps" in our understanding, between children and their parents, between citizens and their government, are the only reasonable result in a society which idolizes specialization. Perhaps it is possible for a man to be really a man as well as a technician or banker or professional sportsman, but there are still only twenty-four hours in the day, and a man cannot be a human being if he spends all of his waking hours chasing success in his profession. *The man who is fluent in the language of his hobby or of his job is not necessarily fluent in the words of life.* He handles easily the technical vocabulary which makes him unique, which makes him a chief of state or a factory foreman, but the language which makes him one with his fellow human beings he may know barely at all. The words *unity* and *uniqueness* obviously have a common origin, but they have long gone their separate ways.

Though we should like to believe in each other, as members of the same family or as citizens of the

same country, we cannot. The vocabulary gap
becomes the "credibility gap." How do we know who
speaks the truth if we speak different languages? We
don't. Even the devout among us recognize that the
population of our nation, like Jerusalem on a feast
day, includes "men from every nation under heav-
en"; even believers have trouble believing each other.
We try so hard to become united that we trample
each other's uniqueness. We straddle the treacherous
line between death together and life in isolation. We
suffocate in dullness or freeze in pride. We conform
to the American Way of Life or rebel against it—or
we crack under the strain of maintaining a public
image no longer consistent with our private beliefs.

The differences of vocabulary among the hearers in
Jerusalem on the feast of Pentecost could not have
been greater than the differences in language or in
divisive technical vocabularies among Americans
today. The miracle in Jerusalem was not that there
were electronic translators available. The miracle
was that, even though only Galileans spoke, each
hearer heard them speaking in his own language.
The miracle was in the willingness of the hearers to
hear as well as in the ability of the speakers to speak.

To find the language which unites all mankind, we
must go back to the beginnings; we must begin with
Adam, or at least with Noah. To find the unifying
language of Judaism, we must go to Moses and
David. To find the unifying language of the earliest

Christian church, we must go to the Evangelists and
to Peter and Paul. In any case, to find the language
which set the stage for a given society or system, we
must go to its origins.

The astrophysicist explores the birth of the stars.
The archaeologist explores the birth of civilizations.
The Supreme Court explores the constitution. But
though the vocabularies of science and sociology and
law may parallel, they divide. *Only one vocabulary
creates unity: the language of the family.*

Without denying the uniqueness of the individual,
the words of a family create unity. Without denying
the uniqueness of each separate child, the words of
God create community. Overcoming the natural disintegration of order, overcoming personal inertia,
overcoming death itself—words create life.

*The work of words is not finished in creation, but
must continue in the maintenance and purposeful
redemption of what has been made. Words themselves, once fallen into disrepute, must be redeemed
and restored to their original brightness and strength.
Words must be made real. They must have meaning
in flesh and blood.* They must have meaning consistent with the evidence of nature. Finally, they
must be allowed to work.

No one denies the language of material power, of
physical love, or of even the aroma of bacon and
coffee in the morning. No one denies the effectiveness

of fears, of hungers, or of warm desires. No one denies the reality of the visible world; few deny the reality of the invisible emotions; but many deny the reality of words. Yet to commit one's life to the service of the Word is in no way to deny the basic reality of the world, nor to deny one's own emotional involvement in it. Devotion to the Word clarifies existence and enriches it, binding one irrevocably to reality.

The world is full of critics who suggest that devotion to a country, to a principle, or even to God, when there is no alternative, is slightly less than honorable; but Life offers no alternative—except death. Having seen, in Jesus, Life, Peter could affirm boldly his choice; having seen in his own existence the seeds of death, modern man might proclaim the same choice: "Lord, to whom shall we go? You have the words of eternal life."

The Life that Peter saw was the perfect wholeness of the spirit and mind and body in Jesus. The death that modern man sees is the disintegration of his own person under the pressures of the time, the disintegration of his family life, and of his whole "civilized" society.

The children of men, born of the will of men, pass their given years on earth—and die. Their natural heredity and the acceptance of their moderately congenial environment grant them this much—but no more. And rational man, considering death as his

natural end, views suicide as the more logical conclusion.

The late American psychiatrist and author, Robert
Lindner, suggests an out, the "instinct of rebellion"
by which, he says, man strives to overcome his "triad
of limitations": heredity, environment, and death.
The nineteenth century Russian, Vladimir Soloviev,
describes a similar triangular prison: nature, sin,
and death. Our bodies indeed rebel against death,
but our minds are not so certain. Soloviev considers
man's two wishes, for immortality and for goodness;
but even the most simpleminded soon sees, as he
points out, (1) that man's goodness doesn't endure,
and (2) that man is unworthy of immortality, and
would therefore be unable to bear it.

Yet Peter's attraction to Jesus was based upon his
fascination with *eternal* life. When we marry, or
when we even begin a new year, we have an opportunity for a *new* life; but *unless we are carried into
it by the right words, the new life soon becomes as
sour as the one before it.* Peter must have seen in
Jesus the possibility of a life of quite a different
nature from his own to have found it so compelling.
He must have seen in Jesus a life worthy of being
lived for all eternity—a sort of life worth living
forever. And Peter, knowing no alternative to the
real life he saw in Jesus, was well on the way to being
born into this new life.

Though the words of Jesus are often an affront to

the rational mind, as the words of eternal life they continue to attract the descendants of workers like Peter and Andrew and of scholars like Nicodemus and Paul. Men still see in Jesus newness of life: not just the same old life for all eternity, but a wholly new kind of life; not even a return to the old Eden of infancy, but a real heaven for grown-ups.

It takes being reborn.

The
Universal
Bloodstream

Truth is not recognized by people en masse. Crowds of common people, we are told in Scripture, heard Jesus gladly; the twelve disciples knew in a general way that this was the man for whom, in their hearts, they had longed; but it took one man, Peter, to focus the desire of them all: "Lord, to whom shall we go? You have the words of eternal life."

Many of the varied heroes of literature share one common characteristic: loneliness. *The surest cause of alienation is to see clearly what those about you have missed or forgotten.* Any child, who during a school recitation suddenly comes upon the right answer long before his classmates, knows perfectly well, from even his best friend, the daggers of envy and hatred. The answers to the greatest questions of life are similarly recognized by just one person out of a crowd. There may be spiritual twins or triplets, or even whole households reborn at one time, but the rebirth which follows the discovery of the words of eternal life is most often single.

14

The words of Jesus which Peter recognized as the key to Life were not exactly secret passwords designed to keep people out. They were, in fact, the most common or universal words Jesus could possibly have spoken, so that hearers from all levels of society and from all times and places have been able to understand them. The compelling authority with which Jesus spoke depended upon two points: he spoke that which he knew, and he spoke that which his hearers knew to be true.

Consider the word *king*, which Jesus used in his parables to mean lord, master of a household or of a people. All of his immediate hearers knew the word. Every younger brother or sister, at least, knows that children are born with rank. Children soon discover that the equality "enlightened" sophisticates teach is an illusion. On the other hand, the word *king* (or *master* or *lord*) is reinforced not only by our knowledge of the past but by our present experience with our nearest neighbor or brother as well. Equality is a good enough word, but it is terribly difficult to make real, whereas a chain of command is one of the surest realities in anyone's life. Thomas Jefferson did not repeal the law of primogeniture.

How much of our total resources of time and wealth and energy do we devote to teaching ideas which cannot be reinforced by some long-term authority, either godly or historical, or even by the witness of our everyday behavior? Was it because

he avoided this pitfall that Jesus was able in three
short years to teach the words that matter for all
eternity? He confined himself to what he knew to be
necessary, eternal, and universally verifiable.

Is it really so amazing that a shepherd leaves
ninety-nine safe sheep to find one that is lost? Is it
really so remarkable that a woman who finds her
lost coin or jewel calls her neighbors to rejoice with
her? Or that a father whose son has left home should
see the returning wanderer while he is still a long
way off?

To common people, who know the everyday language of responsibility of work, of housekeeping, or
of parenthood, these parables are the Truth, and the
Man who spoke them is the Truth Incarnate.

The words *shepherd*, *housewife*, and *father* mean
something that can be grasped, that can be verified
every day. Yet we spend so much of our time teaching
the children of America words like *equality*, *freedom*, or *democracy*—words which not only strain
their comprehension but which often cannot be
verified by experience, either in a family of three or
in a nation of two hundred million. To be the Truth,
words have to have real and durable meanings. Yet
society expects us to trust in ideas which are contrary
to everyday experience. Today's middle-aged parents,
for example, are reaping the folly of the home eco-
nomists' teaching of the 1940s which stressed "democratic" family living.

Conscientious parents teach children about authority in their homes, while the state and the school teach democracy the best six hours of the child's day. Parents teach courtesy toward the weak, while movies and television *and* the government teach firepower under any and all circumstances. Parents teach honest means for honest goals; they teach that freedom is the opportunity (as Helmut Thielicke points out) to do what one *should*—while our whole government preoccupies itself with saving face. In short, we teach at home that fathers are fathers, mothers are mothers, and children are children; we teach that true freedom is the opportunity to be what one is. But freedom is taught in our public life as the opportunity to do whatever one pleases and to be whatever is being sold this week in the marketplace!

There are still "men of the earth," common, universal people who hear the words of Jesus gladly, and for the same reason: he speaks as one having authority. He speaks words that test the credulity far less than the words of current political philosophers or even current theological brainstormers. His words accord with the evidence of several thousand years of witness, and the evidence of our own eyes.

Newspapers tell us that there are young people in "youth ghettos" from New York to San Francisco who are lonely, afraid, hungry, exhausted, and thoroughly ashamed, but who will not go home because "I couldn't go home to my parents after what

I have done to them." Yet the prime word of Jesus, *Father*, is being tested and found to be sound by many a runaway who does come to himself and go home. *The words* equality *or* opportunity *or even* love *endure only if they originate in the one word* Father.

How strange that after all these years the secret of all of Jesus' teaching is still hidden from the wise and prudent but available to every child!

One could study the Gospels computer-fashion and tabulate the particular words Jesus emphasized. Or one could take as a guide the summary he himself gave of his work. Before his death, Jesus talked over his assignment with God, reporting that he had "accomplished the work" God had given him to do. First of all, Jesus could honestly say, "I have made known thy name to the men thou hast given me."

Making known the name of God among the Jews of his day was in itself revolutionary. For people who, out of fear and reverence, never called God by name, it must have seemed an intolerable insolence for Jesus to speak so familiarly of him. Yet in doing exactly this, Jesus says, "I glorified thee on earth." That is to say, God is honored in that his name is made known. And the sacred name which Jesus made known is *Father*. Every other word Jesus brought to men springs from this one word *Father*, for he says further, "I have given them the words which thou gavest me." The whole gospel brought to men for their salvation is summarized in this same word. The essence of Jesus' teaching is simply this:

1) God is *my* Father;
2) As his Son, I welcome you into his household;
3) The Spirit proves the arrangement—it works.

This threefold statement is the lifeblood of the individual believer. It is the universal blood type common to all kinds of believers united in the kingdom of God. It is the code of life passed from one generation of believers to the next.

One doesn't easily see the chemical structure of the genes that encode hair color; one sees the light or dark hair. Neither does one see the spirit of faithful understanding which unites believers; one does, however, hear their words. And one is justified in evaluating their speech by its consistency with their *way* of doing things as well as with *what* they do. It is to be expected that manners and actions will follow thoughts and words. As I think in my heart, so am I.

Our words are a step removed from the thoughts of our hearts, and our deeds are often several more steps away, so that in judging each other's actions we find ample opportunity to practice forgiveness. Nevertheless, the believer who begins his inward thoughts with the word *father*, and who allows his other words to develop from the connotations of *fatherhood*, will find that he too reflects in his life the glory of God. He too will bear witness to the truth in the world. He will have been reborn!

On Being
Born Blind

Children who have observed kittens from birth are aware of the significance of being born blind, and of the excitement of the day when the little pets' eyes open.

The blind kitten learns by touch and smell the properties of his home territory and especially the nature of his mother. He knows what he needs to know to survive as a new kitten; but some change has to be made before he can be on his own even as a fairly young pet, let alone as an adult cat. He has to open his eyes.

Similarly, a believer knows all he needs to know, as a beginner, if he reads or hears the gospel; but if he hopes to grow beyond spiritual infancy he must be really aware of what it says. Unlike kittens, whose eyes seem to open of their own accord, we have to have our eyes opened.

Even though this awakening is as natural in babies as it is in kittens, it is a response, not a self-initiated process; for of what value is a child to himself until he hears the voice of his mother calling him by name? The spiritual awakening of a child, like the eye-opening of the kitten, comes some time after birth, when the child, in the new environment of the world, has learned to respond to the voice of the person who cares for him. Spiritual eye-opening develops not only in the acceptance of love from the mother, but also in a giving of love to the mother. It develops not only in the first and second person relationship between the mother and the child, but soon in a comparable relationship with the father and with siblings. A next giant step in awareness, in eye-opening, is the recognition, even in absence, of the grammatical third person, *he* or *she* or *they*. Then one learns the possessive pronouns, and, like God, learns jealousy as well as ownership. Finally, in a sureness of his own person and of his own possessions, the child learns to respect the identity of another and to share.

Students may advance the art of God-man or man-man relationships to all the conceivable limits of their vocabularies, but they are not likely to go very far beyond the knowledge of God's dealing with men suggested in these personal relationships; for the entire message of the Bible is one of the covenant between a Parent and his children, and between brothers and sisters who are faithful children of one Father. Our pseudosophistication tells us that it can't be that simple; but neither can it possibly be as complicated as the "frontier" studies of man "come of age."

A major miracle in healing the eyes of one born blind is described in great detail by the evangelist John, but no less a miracle occurs when scales of confusion, scales of false values, scales of pretended brilliance fall from the eyes of the wise and prudent so that they may once more become as wide-eyed children. The truly seeing scholar knows on his deathbed, be it at sixty or at ninety years of age, that the truth he sought for his whole lifetime is nothing more or less than the truth he recognized as a child—a child of his father.

Or have today's teachers not had, in their early childhood, parents they could trust? brothers they could love? or maiden aunts who dearly loved them? Have they all been foundlings, whose experience it has been that salvation is to be obtained by hard work? The deep courses in the philosophy of religion and in the research methods in religious thought that fill college catalogues today hardly seem to be organized by men who know anything about grace, or about the simplicity (or the importance) of being born into families and the simple faith learned in faithful homes.

Dulled by such instruction, a great many of us today walk around quite blind. Some of us, born blind, somehow never really opened our eyes; we were afraid to look. Others of us saw clearly up to a given age, when we saw *very* clearly that good eyesight doesn't pay as well as tunnel vision, so we gave up looking all around. Some of us looked where we shouldn't have, or saw those things which, for our age and experience, were too harsh or too overwhelming, and we decided no longer to see. Sometimes we see only in one color or in another; some of us are nearsighted or farsighted, and not a few of us suffer from astigmatism. In general, we see what we want to see, and psychology explains, with a gentle sneer, what early deprivations cause the seeming abnormality, hungry eyeballs.

Blindness is either a limitation, by choice, from within, or a covering up, by oneself or by others, from without. It is a diminishing of reality or a distortion. It is a consequence of too little light or a result of focusing too long on too brilliant a light. And it is more commonly an ailment of later age than of infancy and childhood.

Whatever blindness babies are born with is soon enough overcome by their curiosity, by their joy in learning, and by their parents' delight in teaching. The little one who sees himself reflected in his mother's eyes, who knows himself through her calling his name, and who expresses himself in his response to her love is day by day opening his eyes to a world which can ultimately lead him to all eternity.

Though an optometrist doesn't test eyesight by checking the ears, *the senses are interrelated.* One knows a rose by the smell as well as by the sight, and a pudding by the taste as well as by the texture. *Understanding what one sees is often an essential part of seeing, and therefore tests for vision may be aural and verbal as well as visual.*

Spiritual eyesight is tested by believing and eating and drinking, as well as by hearing and seeing, as well as by being and doing. Jesus presented himself to his followers in as many different guises as possible so that each might, with his own sort of best vision, see him. At the wedding at Cana, he was a joyous guest. At the Passover festival in Jerusalem, he was the passionate Jew, zealous for the sanctity of the temple. To Nicodemus, he was a teacher; to the Samaritan women, a prophet. To a man ill for thirty-eight years, he was the one hope of recovery, and to the father of a dying child, the sure hope of life. By his deeds, many recognized him as a teacher sent from God, for, as Nicodemus said, no one could do such things were God not with him. Most of the people had good enough eyesight to recognize Jesus as a great teacher and a miraculous healer.

For little children, for beginners in faith, this is fine; for grown men and women it is not enough. *To see, one must be hungry. One must hear and touch and see the gospel. One must eat and drink the words of eternal life. One must assimilate the whole vocabulary of God.*

Your fathers, Jesus told his hearers, ate manna in the wilderness and died, but I am the living bread of God which gives life to the world. I give my flesh and blood for you, that you may have eternal life, that, as the Father is in me, so I am in him who eats my flesh and drinks my blood. But to his own chosen disciples Jesus explained specifically, "It is the spirit that gives life, the flesh is of no avail; the words that I have spoken to you are spirit and life."

These descriptions of himself as living water, as living bread, as flesh and blood to be eaten and to be drunk in order to gain eternal life, were indeed "hard sayings" and required either an absolutely infantile faith or a great maturity. The audiences in ancient Jerusalem were probably no more nor less middle-aged than congregations of today, and therefore no more nor less blind than the hearers of the gospel today.

Still, one sees what one chooses to see. One believes and understands what one needs to know. And *even middle-aged blindness can be cured*. It is still the spirit that gives life—the spirit which hungers and thirsts after life, the spirit which recognizes, under the bread and wine, under the body and blood, the true nature of the Father in the eternal Word Incarnate.

For those in love with light and life even the scales of middle-aged propriety, of devotion to outworn duties, of easily shocked sensitivities, can be washed away from the eyes, so that the shining truth becomes again as plain to see as it was in childhood and youth, and quite as certain as it will be in complete maturity.

For those who hunger after eternal life, the living bread and the living water, the flesh and blood of Jesus Christ are all the Word of God. There is no refuge in uncertainty or confusion; there is no excuse in the indigestibility of the vocabulary. The believer simply allows the words of Jesus to live within himself.

One has not truly understood the gospel until that moment when he discovers that, as through the Word the Father is in Jesus, so through the Word Jesus and the Father are in him.

Though I be born blind, "the Holy Ghost has called me by the Gospel, enlightened me with His gifts, sanctified and kept me in the true faith." The call which opens the eyes of the blind is the voice of God, calling his children by name.

The test of sight is faith—faith which enables one to see the Father in Jesus and, seeing, to become one with them.

If *the eyes of the blind are opened by the Word of God*, then it is no exaggeration to say that the Word itself is the greatest of treasures. Not only are the phrases of Holy Scripture a treasure to the believer, but everyday words themselves are precious beyond measure; for *it is through everyday words that God comes to us*, that he reveals himself to us, that he calls us to himself.

Such an evaluation of the Word is no denial of the usefulness of the particular sacraments of the church or of the more general sacramental acts of our daily lives. Nor does one deny the special characteristics by which music or art or drama reveals to us the nature of God. To praise God's Word as the chief means of his grace to man is by no means to deny or devalue his presence in all of creation. *The Word is the man-sized reality by which man may hold fast to the reality of God himself.*

One who is blind to the content of a word is also blind to its importance. The conscience of the man to whom truth is revealed is still captive to the Word of God; unfortunately the blind leader of the blind is not much guided by his conscience. It is of no concern to him that concise, clear statements of belief undergo such frequent metamorphoses even in the church that two children in the same family—let alone parent and child—have scarcely studied a common statement of their faith. It is of no concern to him that the clear expression of specifically enumerated details by a man who loved his "life, goods, fame, child, and wife" becomes in a proper Victorian translation a conglomerate of "mortal life, goods, and kindred" (child and wife can be glossed over, but *goods* remains the same!).

Nor are the blind aware of the peculiar characteristics of particular languages, or of a given language

at a particular stage of its development. The good
ladies who are the first to complain over the tarnish-
ing of the altar silver or the fading of the lectern
hangings are not at all aware of the shift from the
rhythmic, harmonious prose of John Donne's age to
the first grade blitherings of simplifiers of the
liturgy. Nor are all of the agile young men with their
degrees in church music aware of the shift from the
transparent clarity of a simple polyphonic chorale to
the purple fudge of Hollywoodian salvation.

It has been said that a man is truly at home in
the language in which he first knew Jesus Christ. If
this were without exception, there would be no reason
to be concerned with second languages, to be familiar
with art or music beyond our own time and place,
to learn from the secondhand experiences of our
elders. Each one could know Christ in his own
language, in his own mode or coloration, his own
firsthand experience. Each one could know a Christ
strictly limited by his own cell walls—hardly a
Savior large enough to overcome the whole world.

Because one tends to love dearly that which has
been a part of one's childhood, it is only natural to
prefer to worship in one's native tongue; this is surely
most often the language in which one has first known
Christ. On the other hand, a knowledge of Christ
derived from speech depends upon the nature of the
language itself. A language which efficiently describes the assembling of a transistor radio kit is not

necessarily the best language in which to describe the
graciousness and goodness of God. One must at least
choose different words. A language which accurately
distinguishes all aspects of constitutional law is not
necessarily the best language to describe tender
feelings of love or courageous statements of faith.
Furthermore, an age in which all possible shortcuts
and slang expressions are used to develop cynicism
and disbelief is hardly an age in which the contemporary speech will adequately express faith.

A language might truly be rated by its ability to
express the attributes of God, for no language, no art,
is greater than the purpose it serves. A people might
be judged by their steadfastness in the devotion of
their language to the glory of God. *Ultimately, one is
what one thinks. For most of us, this means we are
what we say, and how we say it. One who is aware
of the value of his thoughts cannot afford to be blind
to the words that clothe them.*

What joy and tenderness are expressed in the words
of Job, when, in the last chapter of the book, he
addresses the Lord: "I have heard of thee by the
hearing of the ear: but now mine eye seeth thee."
More outwardly exciting, though no more wonderful,
is the disciples' report to Thomas, after Jesus' Easter
evening appearance: "We have seen the Lord."

Seeing is in itself time-consuming, but enjoying
the wonder of sight is even more so. In only seven

verses John tells us the story of Jesus' noticing and
healing a man born blind; it takes thirty-three verses
for him to describe the aftermath of the miracle. The
former blind man knew exactly what had happened,
and he expressed joy in his new sight as concisely as
Job or as the disciples: "One thing I know, that
though I was blind, now I see." Yet we may be sure
that he spent much time, indeed the rest of his life,
reveling in the wonder of sight.

The Pharisees cast the man out of the temple for
his impudent confession of faith, but it is likely that
he would have been an outcast sooner or later any-
how. *Society has little use for former blind men.
Society has little time to waste on wonder, and even
less on joy.* We know the sufferings of Job and the
arguments concerning them, but we forget so often
his joy: "Now mine eye seeth thee." We review the
stations of the cross, the various incidents of the
passion of Jesus, even the miracle of the resurrection,
but we forget so often the true marvel of Easter
evening: "We have seen the Lord." Like the crowds
and like the rulers of the temple, we examine closely
the reasons for a man's blindness, the technical details
of the healing, and all the opinions pertinent thereto,
but we easily slide over the critical line, "Now I see."

The wandering eye is a time-waster. The playful
eye is a tease. The accurate eye is clever, perhaps, but
potentially dangerous. Only a very exceptional society
can afford men who see for the fun of it; *only a*

very unusual society can tolerate men who see and know the truth. Even fewer societies recognize, let alone honor, a man who, seeing the truth, makes it visible to others. Carried away by every new insight, such a person is too great a risk for the temple or for the school or for the government! The sharp edge of his newly discovered truth cuts too deeply into the status quo, causing the friends who tossed him pennies when he was blind to become his worst enemies now that he sees.

If a first test for sight is faith in what one sees, a second test might well be the willingness with which one receives a new member of the club. A man who himself sees has time to share the joy and wonder of sight with a newcomer; he who sees the truth clearly has nothing to fear from the new man with twenty-twenty vision. The newcomer into any society, the newly sighted man with the fresh approach, is, like Jesus, one who comes for judgment—not that *he* judges, but that the judgment is given on the basis of who sees and who does not see, for a new insight often opens the eyes of the blind and shuts tight the unwilling eyes of those who think they see.

The test of vision for a whole society is its willingness to see—or to accept those who see. A community or a denomination or a particular congregation might well ask itself whether the member with twenty-twenty eyes alienates himself from the majority or whether the group "casts out" the man who sees. In either case, the man who says "Now I see" or "We have seen the Lord" or "I have heard of thee by the hearing of the ear: but now mine eye seeth thee"— this man has no intention of being told by someone else what he is *supposed* to see.

The
Learning
Game

The
Establishment

Rather overpowered by the fun of it all, and not beyond proving himself to be at least a partial image of God, man recreates himself. Or so he thinks. Could God have been as surprised at times by Jesus as earthly parents are by their children? Was it at moments of overwhelming joy and delight that God himself burst the heavens to declare his pleasure in this firstborn Son?

We pretend, under our constitution and therefore by nature, that each of our children is himself. Not Daddy's nose and Mama's hair and Uncle Joe's ears, but himself. And most certainly not the essential personality of one mother-in-law or the other. Neither, in identity-oriented America, are twins twins. (Quintuplets we allow to be quintuplets; it pays.) Each of us must be himself, with his own identity, his own social security number, his own self-evolved democratic principles, and his own private religion. And then the wise among us observe a frightful tendency toward disunity and collect lecture salaries explaining why.

On the other hand, each of us must be in agreement with provincial school systems, with heirarchial churches, and with constitutional governments as defined by the emergencies of the here and now. And Margaret Mead assures us that major nervous disorders can be avoided by recognizing any deviation from *normal* while it is still small enough to correct effectively; for today's Americans have increasingly less tolerance of correctable peculiarities, even of the emotions, than their earlier counterparts.

Fools that we are, we keep on marrying and bearing children with the same stupid defects over and over again. The norm is tall, blond, and willowy, and we keep bearing daughters short, dark, and awkward. The norm is bright, exciting, and popular, and we keep bearing sons slow to start, quiet, and uninvolved. We go on recreating, not exactly ourselves, but bits and pieces of Aunt Susie, Uncle Al, Grandpa Schnurrbart, and sister Eleonore in new configurations.

Yet it is by these little wonders of the world that a man is to be judged. For *the son sees what the father does, and does it too. Or the son sees what the father does, and moves heaven and earth within himself to have no part of it. It depends partly upon the father. And in either case the father is judged by the behavior of the child*—the child who accepts and copies him or who repulses and denies him. Furthermore, the parent is ultimately judged also by the child himself.

Every Saul has his Jonathan, every David his Absalom, and every Paul his faithful and beloved Timothy.

Children are adoptive as well as natural. Even one's own children have a second chance, in maturity, to accept or reject their natural parents; which in turn gives parents the opportunity to live with their children in humility and honesty, or to flee from them in pride. *When the parent cannot accept judgment by the child, it is not always the child who is immature. When a teacher cannot accept criticism by a fresh-eyed student, it is not always the student who is incompetent. And when a national government cannot accept condemnation by its children, it is not always the children who are impudent;* the problem is as often the impudence of psychic rigidity or of senility.

One might suggest that young people look to their elders for acceptance as new members of society, and this is indeed appropriate in terms of the organization of the world. But by the words of Jesus the situation may be reversed: one hopes that the elders will, in forgiveness and love, be found acceptable to the children.

"The Father judges no one, but has given all judgment to the Son. . . . For as the Father has life in himself, so he has granted the Son also to have life in himself, and has given him authority to execute judgment, because he is the Son of man. . . . Do not

think that I shall accuse you to the Father; it is Moses
who accuses you, on whom you set your hope."

Nowhere is this position of Jesus' a denial of the
commandment to place God first, or to honor, as his
earthly counterparts, parents, teachers, and governors. It is only a warning that, as the Father risks
his own honor and glory in the behavior and speech
of the Son, so parents and teachers and governors
risk their good names in the lives of their children,
their pupils, and their citizens.

Furthermore, one who fails to honor the Son fails
to honor the Father from whom he comes. A teacher
who lacks respect for his pupil also fails to respect
the tuition-paying father upon whom his salary
depends. Governments which do not take seriously
the needs of the least of their citizens also fail to take
seriously the Father from whom the citizens derive
life and from whose consent governments derive their
just powers!

We put our trust in the law, in our written constitution. And it is our constitution which condemns us.
A governor or president is not overthrown because of
his gracious words to the voter, but because of his
inability to execute the mandate of the voter in behalf
of the child. The administration which pleads its
courtesy to the father as an excuse for disservice to
his son fails in its chief duty. For *the minimum service of any law is to provide a system assuring on-
going stability, not current grandeur*. Of how many

governments in the world can it be said that the
welfare of the young of every *niveau* is the chief
concern of the state?

Ultimately, one is judged by the future—even,
parasitically, consumed by the future. One is judged
by progression, not by present satisfaction. The
present is indeed not my own work; it is what I have
received from my elders. I am judged, therefore, not
by what I do at any given moment, but by what I am
able to pass on to my children; not, therefore, by how
I honor or defend my peers, who are no more worthy
of honor than I (for much of what they have has also
originated with others), but by how I serve our various children and secure their future.

Children may not only be adopted by anxious
parents; they may quite reasonably adopt parents of
their own. And they do: movie queens, gangster-
heroes, rabble-rousers, successful drunks, best-dressed
socialites, and spectacular politicians. Or they may
accept the proffered adoption by God as the normal
extension of earthly parenthood. Then, having chosen
or having been chosen, the son does that which he
sees his "father" do.

Of a generation of which it might be said that every
color or race or age is preoccupied with its own existence, one might also say, with Paul, "Men shall be
lovers of their own selves, . . . ever learning, and
never able to come to the knowledge of the truth."

Of a generation of which it might be said that its scientific understanding is almost beyond cataloging, one might say that it is close to only one aspect of the knowledge of truth: death. For in the end nothing is as appealing to the man in love with his own intellect as suicide. But in the meantime he has already squandered a lifetime, ever learning, yet completely bypassing the truth.

Some schools teach religion, but not faith; biblical literature, but not belief; contemporary Christian thought, but not eternal life. Our scientific institutes teach recognition and accumulation of facts, but not wonder. Our classes in the fine arts, in some cases, teach absurdity in sound and sight, but not joy. And in departments of languages, how many vocabularies are taught, being systematically stripped of their saving glory: inner meaning? For so often teachers are lovers of teachers, psychologists lovers of psychologists, and guidance counselors lovers of guidance counselors. And mothers are lovers of mothers, fathers of fathers, and children of children. All of them "ever learning and never able to come to the knowledge of the truth."

For truth requires knowledge—primarily self-knowledge, the quiet awareness of what one does not know, and secondarily the knowledge of others and of self in relation to others. The endless multiplication of assignments, of recitations, of examinations and term papers impresses only those with the ability to fool themselves. Thus gifted, who is able to arrive at a knowledge of truth?

Biochemical experiments designed to test a thesis may be performed *in vitro* or *in vivo*, dead or alive. A young child who knows the living truth of a faithful family situation is not much impressed by the pseudo-life of artificial love in teaching situations in glass-walled first-grade classrooms. Nor is he much impressed by pretense in school systems where one omniscient mother-substitute presumes to teach in one classroom a core curriculum covering all branches of knowledge of all ages of the universe. Nor is the tenth-grader impressed by the English specialist who pretends to cover in one year, via literature, not only the seven ages of man but also the complete history of Western civilization. In all of these cases, the superintendent is impressed, and perhaps even one's fellow teachers; but not the student, or the parent, who is obliged to produce the goods. Such teachers might take to heart one gem of our elders: From a distance one fools many people; up close, one fools only oneself.

A child who has learned *in vivo*, in his parents' home, respect for reality is not easily fooled. What he learns in school, in public, is, unfortunately, that *the business of the world is frequently conducted by people whose preoccupation is fooling each other*. In a day in which information is tested, recorded, and manipulated by machinery to insure its accuracy, he

sees that people live more and more by their ability
to fool themselves. And when he grows up, when he
learns to love himself more than he loves the truth,
he too may play the game.

He will learn the psychology of the big lie: not to
see what the eye sees, not to hear what the ear hears,
not to know what the heart feels. He will learn to hear
and see what is supposed to be heard and seen, and
in spite of some sixteen to twenty years of education
"to teach him to think for himself" he will learn to
think what is being thought. He will also learn the
meaning of schizophrenia, of repressed hatreds ex-
ploding in vengeful violence, and of miserable under-
confidence and ineptness washed in tears of bewilder-
ment.

He has lost his evenings of recreation, his holy
days of worship and freedom; he has lost a whole
childhood of wonder and joy; he has joined the ranks
of those who are ever learning and never able to
know the truth.

Or else he holds erect within himself the image of a
God who will not be hurried and whose first alle-
giance is not to the blue and orange of East-West
High School, but to Truth.

Educators have long flimflammed American students and parents with the doctrine that one teaches
the pupil, not the subject; that a good teacher loves
the children, not the Latin or the arithmetic. Though
clever apologists point out that of course one can't

teach the subject without the pupil, or vice versa, real harm has already been done. We have had at least a full generation in many areas in America during which teachers have fed children the pap of their own self-importance and have forgotten to nourish their souls on truth.

I am not impressed. And neither, apparently, are thousands of frustrated young people in America, to whom a distant war is not the chief cause of distress, but merely the last straw.

The preoccupation with self and the corresponding loss of contact with the truth is hardly a new problem, nor is it a specific one; but there have been times and there have been places where truth has triumphed sufficiently over self-love to give its followers a glimpse of their real "native land." Those who grew up in such an environment had hopes of preserving it for their children, or of even spreading it to benefit others. They seem to have been outvoted.

Truth is not available to those who prefer absolute freedom. A choice must be made. One integrates one's life in allegiance to the truth, or one, in self-love, dissipates it in the pride of ever learning.

There is more to be learned from America's Southwest than the idolizing of the fast-drawing sheriff. An important lesson is to be learned from the digs in various dried-out canyons: a people will not survive if it is unable, because of severe drought or severe winter, to hold on from one year to another. A civilization is wiped out if it is able to build for only one season; a culture dies if it builds for only one generation.

A man builds the future for his child. The child builds the future for his adult life. Life builds the future for eternity. This is all normal and reasonable; but how easily the program is upset by emergencies in an individual life, let alone by emergencies on a national scale, when sudden demands are so expensive that the future is almost wiped out.

The collapse of a dynasty may abort the future; but it is almost certain to bury the past. Youth has the "life," the strength, to survive and, in survival itself, to pass judgment on the fathers.

Even where society passes from one generation to the next peaceably, *youth "judges" in its work, as the "underdog" generation, in bringing about correction of felt wrongs.* Where such "wrongs" are obvious injustices or intentional cruelties, it is no wonder that the judgment is harsh; but the less obvious wrongs of setting pretentious standards, or of giving inadequate support, or of taking away the expected support while maintaining or increasing the demands—these wrongs are every bit as detrimental. They are even more dangerous for their being the less apparent. An established generation, believing in its own deceits and busy with its own survival, is not likely to take kindly the criticisms of young people stretched thin between the scant aid offered them by society and the tremendous deeds expected of them. *One can rightly ask youth what it will do for its country, but youth is also right to ask what its country has done and will do for it.*

The young who call for justice for the poor and mercy and kindness toward the lowly, for respect for honest workmanship and reward for honest labor; the young who withdraw their cooperation from government for, by, and of the interrelated wealth of war and industry; the young who demand of men preaching faith that they themselves be faithful—these young people are paraphrasing Isaiah and Amos and Jeremiah whether they know it or not. Not only is the available cloud of witnesses, assembling from the graves to back clamorous youth, great in number; it is also great in the names of those prophets of all time who defied power for the sake of truth.

Jesus does not indicate a distinction between young and old, between black and white, or even between living and dead. The distinction is rather between those who have done good and those who have done evil, between believers in truth and believers in power, money, and pragmatism, in romantic love, security, success, happiness, and prestige—all of which may be sweet at the moment but which do not secure the future for one's children.

Societies in the relative Edens of some of the South

Sea Islands may with little forethought have developed a system of near balance among men, women, and children, but more difficult climates and more intensely populated areas require more specific guidance. For beings made in the image of God, it seems only reasonable to follow his pattern of behavior: the son, if he is wise, still does what he sees the Father do. And what does the Father do?

The Father bases his whole system on the concept that salvation is in the Son, and that, on earth, the child matters, and because of the child, the mother, and for the sake of both, the father. The principle set out by God still holds: the master is the servant of all; each is for the service of the other.

To almost every man is given the experience of fatherhood. From this firsthand knowledge of life he is able to learn the essentials of educational psychology and method, the underlying facts of government based on mutual respect, and the laws of supply and demand. From his own engagement in the task of being a father he learns the vocabulary of life.

The words of eternal life for which Peter longed are still the words of Jesus: the simple, everyday words of the relationships of parents to children, of masters to servants, of governments to peoples. One sees their verification in one's own life, sometimes from one point of view, as a son, a servant, a citizen, and at other times as a parent, a master, or a governor.

One sees their verification in their fruitfulness, in their effectiveness, in their power.

If the evidence of one's own experience is not enough, then consider the power of words such as *love*, *faithfulness*, and *sensitivity*, which either lift young people to the highest levels of creativity or which, in their nonfulfillment, drive them to despair. If the evidence of adolescents driven to spiritual or physical suicide by trying to reach impossible standards and at the same time remain faithful to their ideals; if the evidence of youth who feed and warm and comfort each other when the system says simply that they've failed; if the evidence of brave young men who refuse to take life in the defense of adult pride— if this evidence is not the medium through which society understands the words of life, the problem is not necessarily with youth.

One may "belong"; one's ancestors may have either arrived on the first boat or met the boat; but he who thinks to supercede, by birth or rank or money, the ultimate judgment of history, being satisfied with the flattery of his peers, is welcome to his illusion. He may buy and assemble about him the young people who prefer his well-established company: they will prove faithful to his way of life.

The others have already been bought, and no price can take them out of the courts of Truth.

The
Interior
Fatherland

The Boston cartoonist Dahl presents us with a remarkable sketch of the inner depths of a streetcar, the "terra incognita" avoided with fear and trembling by the passengers who prefer the security of being close to the front or back door.

There have been times and places in America when our most private physical activities were similarly terra incognita to the public, whereas our deepest and most vital thoughts about God were well known. Even so short a time ago as before World War II, very few of us expected a day when our verbal public expression of the relationship between God and man would be so disdained, and our most intimate physical expression of this relationship so flagrantly displayed. The most casual observation of human nature teaches that nothing shows so clearly in the life of a man as that which he is most anxious to hide or to deny. The difference is that when one openly admits the truth it is less harmful than when it is repressed, to explode later in its own little way.

Is it our public denial of the relationship of love
between God and man that necessitates our violent
and compulsive exhibitionism of the processes of love
between two human beings? Is it our rejection of the
proffered relationship of love between God and a
whole nation that compels our nation to exhibit its
love for its fellow nations by arming them to the
teeth and by defoliating, burning, and irradiating
their territories? Is it a nation's rejection of its own
terra incognita that drives it to explore the bottom
of the sea or outer space?

This shift in privacy, from a public declaration of
fear, love, and trust in God, to a public declaration
of fear, love, and trust in each other, would not be
so frightening were it possible for us to have both;
but in trying to juggle a love for God and an equal
love for man, we are likely to end up with neither.
So today we build our house on the sands of public
opinion polls and wonder why it keeps falling apart.
It is with some justification that *one feels safer near*
the doors of the streetcar than in the depths of the
interior, near our surface pretensions rather than in
the realities of our hearts.

Freedom, like certain promotions in the army, is
based on remaining inconspicuous, on very carefully
doing and saying nothing. The simplest deed or word
is a commitment made, a stand taken. One becomes
the prisoner of the moment just past. We are partic-

ularly prisoners of our own speech. If we speak of details, the accumulation becomes unbearable. If we speak in generalities, the limitations become unendurable. We must categorize to make life manageable, but in such a way that important distinctions survive. Freedom is hardly the opportunity to lose all of one's individuality in the mass—though those who are comfortable with the generalization, the American Way of Life, are free to do so.

To the mind of the satisfied, the interior of the heart of the malcontent is indeed terra incognita. As long as he himself is not bothered, the man who is satisfied with his life couldn't care less; but when he feels threatened by underground rumblings, when he sees his own personal timetable endangered, or his private little games about to be exposed, he does care. He just doesn't understand. He changes his makeup, his eyeglasses, his hairstyle; he stabilizes all the externals; he confirms his devotion to reality, to the status quo; and he wonders, with no particular determination to find out, why he is so misunderstood. The terra incognita of the interior is not for him.

Not for him is that country of the Book called by Heinrich Heine the Portable Fatherland. Not for him is the invisible nation of believers in God. Not for him is the insignificant interior of one man's conscience. And most certainly not for him is the attitude of an Ibsen in exile, who writes to his mother-in-law at home that he cannot allow his son to grow up in a country where the people prefer being Englishmen to being human beings.

The individual in America is no more "free" of the acts of his government, good or bad, than the individual of Nazi Germany or of the Soviet Union. And he is the less free for having been assured that he is free. The American Way of Life, the Constitution of the United States, the Bill of Rights, for all their talk of freedom, are not worthy of the *first* fear, love, and trust of the heart of man. Freedom is possible only "under God," its author. Any other freedom is a lie.

What does the terra incognita, the interior fatherland of the spirit, have that the United States of America lacks? For one thing, real freedom—freedom from fear, freedom from loneliness, freedom from worry, freedom from death. It has stability without sacrificing potential; community without sacrificing identity; warmth without sacrificing reason; and power without sacrificing love.

It demands allegiance, but offers purpose and reward. It demands courage, but offers strength and comradeship. It demands worship, but offers a Lord worthy to be worshiped. Whatever the cost, it offers joy!

It offers its children of all ages eternal youth, the secret of eternal happiness, and the sweet water of eternal life: shared gratitude.

Seeing
It
Through

No game in life is so respected as the game called
Seeing It Through. No performance is so essential as
finishing what one has begun. No pride is so satisfy-
ing as that derived from overcoming every obstacle
until death itself.

> Cannon to right of them,
> Cannon to left of them . . . .

Six hundred or one, one finishes that which is begun.
One is what one is.

Wars rage, hurricanes roar, assassins shoot, and
college admissions boards regret to inform you. The
church treasurer calls to your attention the impend-
ing deficit, and the President of the United States
sends greetings. Through it all, one remains faithful:
one remains what one is.

Maturity consists, partially at least, in recognizing
and accepting the consequences of one's behavior,
even of one's existence. The victory is to him who
endures—preferably within the law, but in any case
dependent upon the law. One learns the rules and

expects to play the game accordingly, and the essential rule is survival.

Into the valley of death . . . .

The only sure law is that man, putting his trust in law today, dies by the law tomorrow. *The prison of one's past grants no pardons.* Man enters life, conforms to the rules of the jail, and is carried out. He hears of occasional reprieves or escapes, but to the aging prisoner, knowing only the tapping on the walls of his maximum security cell and the footsteps in the dark hall, these are as likely as not rumors and illusions. There is a certain honor in seeing one's imprisonment through, and no dishonor in dying quietly. Early, one thinks to survive by cooperative obedience and later, by cleverness; but ultimately the walls close in. Not without some comfort, one is aware that the jailers themselves are no less walled in. And not without some comfort, one is aware that the same law of death applies no less to those outside one's own particular prison.

The condemnation of his past, of what he has done and of what he has not done, is carried by every man within his own cell walls. Only the walking dead are spared: only those people and those nations which continue operating efficiently day after day, year after year, not knowing. Knowing the rules, to be sure; knowing the origins of peoples, the properties of matter and energy, the observable causes of observed effects; forever learning and never arriving at the knowledge of truth.

The scribes and the lawyers of our day, who, having used "the words" for their own meager glories, having used "reason" for their own manipulations, arrive only at the knowledge of death—with, at most, a pseudoheroic "nevertheless."

If the wages of sin is death, may not one take as a clue to an individual tragedy or to a national disaster the relationship between the two? The one doesn't exist without the other. To persons less sophisticated than Jean-Paul Sartre, the word is life, not the "nevertheless" response of a circulatory system in which the spirit has failed to ignite. To persons less confident than Lyndon Johnson, reason is life, not the excuse for the escalation of death. *Death is the wage of the misuse of the word*, of the misuse of the reason, as well as the wage of the dishonoring of the body.

A precocious child who learns that words can be used to manipulate those who love him, to devastate the less gifted about him, can be expected, for all his verbal maturity or political astuteness, to face imprisonment in his infantile self. Any common man who acknowledges, by the most common procedures, his wife and their children, arrives at the knowledge of truth long before the aging child, still building pretentious houses with his verbal flashcards. Death is as surely the imprisonment of arrested growth as it is the stoppage of the heart and lungs.

Death is also the certain consequence of the misuse of reason, of the forceful and charming ability to present one's own side of the story as though there were no alternatives. And persons who allow themselves to be misled by such lopsided views, even when they have chosen the better of two questionable alternatives, may nevertheless expect to experience that alienation from the community of life which results in death.

Man has no inherent right to teach a child words, without teaching him, in reference to the Word, their proper usage. Man has no right to present, to a populace, reason out of context.

So each man clings desperately to the prison of the winning techniques of his past. He is what he is. Having succeeded at seven or at thirty-four or at sixteen, he chooses that single moment to be the straitjacket of the rest of his life, the skin in which the spirit suffocates and the organs decay.

The dishonoring of any one part of a man brings about the ruin of the whole. Misused words and ideas are as fatal as misused hands and feet or stomachs or lungs. And the skin, which was meant as a dress to unify the whole, to protect the vital parts, to sense and enjoy the messages of nature and of one's companions—this flesh becomes the burdensome prisonhouse of death.

The victories achieved by forcing one's mind or body on and on, in spite of everything, are hardly worth the cost in misery and decay; for what financial or critical or political victory is worth the scorn of the future?

Prisons of stone may once more open their doors to the light of the community of life; but prisons of the mind only deepen the isolation. Words are the key to the prison, and reason is the guide to victory, but only if the words are used in an awareness of their sanctity, and only if the reason follows the mind of God. Then the prison of my skin is transformed into the wedding dress of the incarnate child of God.

The people who believe that by their own reason and strength they can see life through are playing games. Unfortunately they deserve their final isolation, for the harm that they do to others by their example is all out of proportion to whatever benefits they themselves derive. The decisions as to which tasks in life one must finish, as to which task is for whom, or as to the right time and place for a particular purpose—these decisions are too important to be made without considering the example and instruction of God himself: "Wash you, make you clean; put away the evil of your doings from before mine eyes; cease to do evil; Learn to do well; seek judgment, relieve the oppressed, judge the fatherless, plead for the widow. Come now, and let us reason together, saith the Lord: though your sins be as scarlet, they shall be as white as snow; though they be red like crimson, they shall be as wool. If ye be willing and obedient, ye shall eat the good of the land. But if ye refuse and rebel, ye shall be devoured with the sword; for the mouth of the Lord hath spoken it."

Survival
by
Singles

As remarkable as the Ten Commandments themselves are God's "asides," which indicate not only the whys and wherefores but, in one case at least, the motivation for the whole system of law: "For I the Lord thy God am a jealous God, visiting the iniquity of the fathers upon the children unto the third and fourth generation of them that hate me; And shewing mercy unto thousands of them that love me, and keep my commandments."

God's world is a world where jealousy has an honored place, where jealousy is a servant, not a master; and how hard it is for the children of God to endure in a world where jealousy is regarded mainly as a horrible fault to be overcome. Possessiveness is similarly a characteristic which, especially in a mother, is regarded as a heinous sin. Both jealousy and possessiveness war against our publicly declared virtues of independence and freedom, and hence must be overcome. Yet man was made in the image of One who says, "I am a jealous God" and who says,

57

"They shall be my people, and I shall be their God."

In the face of those who worship ultimate wisdom or infinite reason or the first cause or the last catastrophe, God still says, in straightforward personal, possessive pronouns: I shall be *their* God; they shall be *my* people, for I the Lord *thy* God am a jealous God.

The measurers and the logicians want to measure and reason out the existence of God; but God is not so enamored of systems and sciences and hierarchies. God is in love with man, and to man who worships as god a plethora of charts and truth tables God says, "I am a jealous God."

One has only to hear the cry of a young man from a perfectly lovely, well-to-do, but unbelieving family —the cry of frustration in his being unable even to begin to believe—to know how tragically true is the conclusion of this statement: ". . . a jealous God, visiting the iniquity of the fathers upon the children unto the third and fourth generation of them that hate me."

The whole setting of the Ten Commandments is negative. God is not only jealous; God is smart. He knows that love consists in intentional avoidance of evil as well as in the positive pursuit of good. To our plaintive cry, "I didn't mean to," he replies: "You have to mean not to!" *The iniquity which is passed from generation to generation is, if nothing more, the cumulative weight of the consequences of our*

unintentional drifting away from good as well as the
consequences of our deliberate evil; but taken all
together, the iniquity is the depersonalization of God.
One doesn't "mean to" deny or redesign God. One
has to mean not to!

This hereditary-seeming sin is not God's last word
on the subject. He is also a jealous God, "shewing
mercy unto thousands of them that love me, and keep
my commandments." The significant point is that,
while the curse passes on and on through families,
the mercy comes to thousands of them that (individ-
ually) love him and keep his commandments, beginning and ending with the first pronouncement: *I* am
the Lord *your* God.

En masse it is so easy to drift, to slide away. Singly
one believes.

Singly one believes; but singly one is lonely, disappointed, and often frightened. Belief in God is not
easy to sustain without belief in at least one other
person.

Alone, one goes out into the wilderness with the
prayer of Elijah on one's lips: "It is enough; now,
O Lord, take away my life; for I am not better than
my fathers."

Alone, one writes books about the stranger, the
Steppenwolf, the outsider; for, alone, one is jealous
for one's own individuality, or, like Elijah, "very
jealous for the Lord God of hosts: for the children of
Israel have forsaken thy covenant, thrown down

thine altars, and slain thy prophets with the sword; and I, even I only, am left; and they seek my life, to take it away."

God comes to us in bread and water in the wilderness; he comes to us in the strong wind and in the earthquake and in fire. Alone, in the wilderness, hiding in a cave, or out on the raw mountainside, one prepares one's mind to receive the voice of God. Alone, one is able to state one's situation before God.

The man of God, made in his image, is, like the jealous God himself, moved by feelings: he is concerned for the honor of the Name of the Lord God of Hosts, he is disappointed in those who reject the Name, he is alienated from those about him who follow Mars or Bacchus or even Minerva instead, and he would so gladly go off by himself and die quietly.

Good teacher that he is, God's first response is a question. He insists that the man clearly state his case. No matter on which word the accent falls, the question is a guide to the answer: "What *doest* thou here, Elijah?" or "What doest *thou* here?" or "What doest thou *here*?" And, like Elijah, one offers the mass condemnation of one's own contemporaries.

One may of course stay on the rugged mountainside or in the wilderness: staying aloof has its own rewards, arrested development being one of them. Or one may obey the voice of God: obeying has its satisfactions, too, the knowledge that one is *not* alone being one of them. God does not leave his children comfortless. The command "Go, return . . ." is followed by the reminder that the one man, Elisha, is worthy to take over Elijah's exhausting work, and by the assurance that there is still a faithful remnant—"underground," perhaps, but faithful—of "seven thousand in Israel, all the knees which have not bowed unto Baal, and every mouth which hath not kissed him." For the Lord is a jealous God, "shewing mercy unto thousands of them" that love him and keep his commandments.

Seven thousand men in Israel who had *not* worshiped Baal, gathered together in one place, would have been hard to miss; but in a day when the head of state himself, Ahab, in the company of his infamous little queen, set up altars to Baal and "did more to provoke the Lord God of Israel to anger than all the kings of Israel that were before him," it is no wonder that the seven thousand were scattered into invisibility. Yet, Ahab and Jezebel notwithstanding, seven thousand were recognized by God as faithful.

Every en masse condemnation in Scripture concludes ultimately with the promise of salvation. The work of man builds mighty armies of destruction and great hierarchies of conceit, but the Lord builds by holding back the hand of his chosen from foolishness, until the right moment comes to reveal his purpose: "*I* have left me seven thousand." "And *I* will gather the remnant of my flock out of all countries whither *I* have driven them, and will bring them again to their folds; and they shall be fruitful and increase." "Yet will *I* leave a remnant, that ye may have some that shall escape the sword among the nations, when ye shall be scattered through the countries." "Except the *Lord* of Sabaoth had left us a seed, we had been as Sodom, and been made like unto Gomorrha."

In Jesus' day in Jerusalem, there were worshipers of their own personal Baals—power, money, self. There were those so preoccupied with maintaining their own time schedule of success that they tolerated no interference from God himself. Even when they were moved to believe in him, having seen his power in his obvious miracles or in the equally striking "cleansing" of the temple, Jesus knew better than to place his confidence in them. He knew all men; he needed no one to warn him about so-called human nature. John writes, "He knew what was in man."

Jesus had called out from the whole of the people twelve very special friends to whom he *did* entrust himself; but, as for the others, he set into motion a system of elimination that would leave nothing but a remnant, a miserable little heap. He went into the temple like a Harvard freshman: articulate, full of "hard sayings," and nothing if not contrary! In the ordained and established house of worship, he called out, in effect, "You are either the sons of *my* Father in heaven, or the sons of *your* father."

Two sorts of people get his message: the ones who hate him for making the distinction so clear, and the ones who thank him for reassuring them of what they have always known. One by one, the latter respond. One by one, the little crowd grows, not only in numbers, but in joy—much to the annoyance of their "superiors." The Son of man persists in eating and drinking, in assuming that the institution was made for man, not man for the institution. The elders rightly know that this is not the attitude which preserves a profitable way of life. The maintenance of law and order on so grand a scale demands serious work, not the excitement of an itinerant preacher and healer.

It is not without gratitude for the efforts of others that youth and those elders whose youth is renewable even today refuse to take too seriously the demands of church and state: the children of the bridechamber have other things to do, like eat and drink and light their lamps and sing! The choice is made.

The Lord retains for himself a remnant: fools who leave profitable fisheries, fools who embarrass their well-placed friends, fools who sing in prison. Not much of a crowd, perhaps, but a "seed."

Sodom and Gomorrah go their own way, and Capernaum is leveled; the temple falls, the governor's palace falls, and kingdoms and empires, whatever they are called, are still falling.

Ten lepers are offered cleansing; ten lepers show

themselves to the priests; ten lepers fulfill the law; and one, returning to give thanks, finds life.

One ruler of the Jews, one teacher of Israel, Nicodemus, is born anew.

One prophet is rescued in the wilderness.

Royal seals can be forged, clothing can be duplicated, and faces can be made up. From appearances alone, one can never be too sure whether pretenders are disguised as royalty or royalty is hidden in order to pass unknown among the common people. *A prince who chooses to study firsthand the life of his subjects, by living among them, may enjoy being accepted as their peer, but one would hope that his manner, if not his appearance, would soon give him away.*

If the visit is simply a game, or even a fact-finding mission, there is no reason for his identity to be known; but if he is on a mission to bring information, then he must make contact with those who are to receive it and he must by some means verify his identity, for their sake as well as for his own, and for the sake of the mission.

The survival of Elijah in the wilderness and of Nicodemus in the deadwood of the law depended upon making successful contacts. To recognize the still, small voice as the voice of God, Elijah had to have already some familiarity not only with the sound of the voice, but with the sort of ideas it would express as well. To recognize that Jesus came from

God, Nicodemus had to have already some familiarity with the nature and behavior of God. God speaks reassuringly; God is at one and the same time merciful and just, as well as omnipotent.

One wonders how many times a day and in how many places or in how many hearts God visits, under various covers, and is unrecognized, not because of the cleverness of the disguise, but because of the unfamiliarity of earthlings with his way of speaking or doing a thing, as well as with what he says and does.

Friends
of the
Bridegroom

Paintings of Mary with Jesus and John the Baptist as little babies may indicate, by the positions of the children or by some symbol each holds, which little boy is Jesus and which is John; but, as far as the babies themselves are concerned, one could just as easily be the other. As "kinsmen," Jesus and John might have resembled one another closely, or not at all. The distinguishing characteristic was the role each was to fill.

John, even though he surely knew the story of his own remarkable birth, had no illusions about his rank. This prophet of the Most High, this prophet of the Dayspring from on high, may have, in his sorrowful imprisonment, wanted the reassurance that Jesus was truly the One who was to come; but never for a moment did John entertain the illusion that he himself was the Savior of the world, the Bridegroom for whom all creation waited. Was it for this reason that Jesus assured the crowds about him that, of those born of women, none was greater than John?

This greatness—knowing what one is not—is also available to the "least in the kingdom of God."

The bride is quite a prize, and many a *friend* of the bridegroom has presumed to be what he is not. Those entrusted with responsibility for the care and education of the bride have often forgotten that the bridegroom is on his way and expects their preparations to be not only adequate but proper!

John, on the other hand, knew perfectly well that the bride, who for a short while was in his hands, was the bride of another. He was prepared, with an absolutely clean conscience, to present her to the awaited bridegroom, and to rejoice in his coming. "Therefore," he could say, "this joy of mine is full."

The bride too sometimes tires of waiting. She asks of one, and then of another, "Who are you? . . . Are you Elijah? . . . Are you the prophet?" Are you, whoever you are, the one person on earth through whom I am to be redeemed? She seeks where reason (but not necessarily experience) tells her he should be found, and not infrequently she finds herself seriously entangled with hierarchies and constitutions instead of embraced by love. The prize of her virginity is often a little too much for the friends of the bridegroom, but when they have built their temples of love, their palaces, and their administrative chambers, little Mary Susan has slipped away, and they are left with Isaiah's "haughty daughters of Zion," as indecent as themselves.

*The sin of the woman whose honor has been vio-
lated is not that she "committed adultery," but that
she did not cry out*, that she allowed herself to be
taken without exacting a prior contract for the full
price!

The sin of the poor man whose self-respect has
been sold for bread is not that he was hungry and ate
the bread, but that he did not, by his virtue, shame
the salesman.

The sin of the layman whose individual glory has
been sold for "community" is not that he, in his
loneliness, joined the congregation, but that he did
not by his faith defend his own soul.

"I pray Thee that Thou wouldst forgive me all my
sins where I have done wrong," especially the sin of
having sold myself without exacting the full price
for a child of God—sold to the partner in marriage,
to the government, to the church.

The sin, in general, of the "second-class citizen"—
woman, poor man, layman, amateur or student,
employee or serf—is not that he entered into a contract or covenant for security but that he sold himself
too cheaply; for *one's life is determined by the value
one places upon it.*

Sin is being born second—relative to one's parents,
to one's older brother, to one's husband or wife, to
one's teachers and friends, and finally to one's God.
If one category doesn't apply, another does. Those to
whom the term *original sin* is so painful might there-

fore consider instead the doctrine of universal—or catholic—sin.

To be applicable, salvation must also be universal. From the humblest acceptance of a wife or husband as one's own to the most joyous acknowledgment of the relationship of love between God and man, salvation *is* universal. The faith that enables one to believe the Word of God is of the same essence as the faith which enables a young child to believe his older brother or his parents. And the confidence and freedom one knows among friends at work or at school is a preview of the freedom from jealousies and fears that prevails in the kingdom of God.

Sin is universal, and salvation is universal; but still one must marry the bridegroom, and not settle in impatience for any of his lesser friends.

Jonathan and David might well be considered prototypes of John the Baptist and Jesus. Like John, Jonathan knew that a change in dynasty was imminent; he knew that the alliance between the house of Saul and the children of Israel might have sufficed to establish the kingdom, but that it was not the "marriage" which was to last forever. The Spirit of God had quite obviously departed from Saul and had gone to be with David.

To speak of marriage, one must also consider the attitude of the bride. Saul had pleased and delighted the kingdom, for "there was none like him among the people." Furthermore, the dynasty itself seemed assured in the popularity of Jonathan. The people had been hungry for a king, for someone to husband it, to care for and defend it, and Saul had begun well. But, whether the bride is aware of false starts or not, there is a time for a change in the dynasty, a time for a change in the priesthood, a time for a change in the one man himself who should occupy the heart of the bride. And the change comes from within.

It had been a member of the pharaoh's immediate household who had brought about a sudden shift in the affairs of slave-rich Egypt. The young armor-bearer and companion to the king, and sworn friend to the heir to the throne, succeeded Saul. And the son of a righteous priest and a faithful daughter of Aaron declared the establishment of the new priesthood.

Reluctant though the bride may be, roughly as she must sometimes be torn from the bed of the pretender, the spokesman for the bridegroom does not fail. Moses carried the people from slavery in Egypt to nationhood in Canaan. Jonathan, and even foolish little Michal, preserved the life of the founder of the eternal dynasty of Israel. And John the Baptist transferred the allegiance of his followers from the Levitical lamb of sacrifice to the Lamb of God himself. For neither the pharaoh nor Saul nor Levi was an adequate husband for the bride.

The woman of Samaria who met Jesus at the well had the same problem. One who hungers and thirsts after righteousness is not satisfied with less. In one's loneliness, one puts faith first in one man's promise and then in another's. It isn't a matter of having had five husbands; in truth, to have five or six husbands with whom spiritual consummation is impossible is to have no husband.

To one seeking a prestigious name, perhaps husband number one had been the answer; to one seeking wealth, perhaps husband number two; to one seeking political power, husband number three. One learns from a series of disappointments. Had the Samaritan woman sought later the virtues of maturity in number four, or respectability in number five, or even faithfulness in number six, even these would have been no assurance of life. She had made quite a row of mistakes, but it could hardly be said that, in playing with fire, she had been burned. It is quite unlikely that she had been playing with fire at all. Oh, fire *she* seemed to have. She surely must have been attractive; a woman hungry and thirsty for life always is. It's just that it takes a man to be worthy of her; and apparently numbers one through five hadn't caught fire!

So many women marry once or six times with the illusion that, because a man breathes in and out on a regular basis, life is there; just as a nation hopes that a crown on a man's head makes him a king, or a book in a man's hand makes him a judge.

The worm in each man's life, like young Moses in the court of the pharaoh, like Jonathan at the table of Saul, like John in the house of Levi, is in his own household—perhaps in his own bed.

The bride is not to be had for the physical consummation, for the legal manipulation, or for the financial agreements. Whether she leaves a pseudo-husband with tears of regret or with joyous abandon, she marries, in truth, only one man: the man who matches the fiery desire of her own soul with the water of life, the bridegroom—not even his best friend.

The Axe
at the
Root of the Tree

No psalm of David's is more moving than the lament
he sang upon the death of Saul and of Jonathan: "The
beauty of Israel is slain upon thy high places: how
are the mighty fallen! . . . Saul and Jonathan were
lovely and pleasant in their lives, and in their death
they were not divided: they were swifter than eagles,
they were stronger than lions. . . . I am distressed
for thee, my brother Jonathan: very pleasant hast
thou been unto me: thy love to me was wonderful,
passing the love of women. How are the mighty
fallen, and the weapons of war perished!"

No act of David's is more representative of the God
whom he cherished in his heart than his remem-
brance, when he at last reigned over all Israel, of his
predecessor, of his brother: "Is there yet any that
is left of the house of Saul, that I may show him
kindness for Jonathan's sake?" In no other way did
David show more clearly that the Spirit of God was
upon him than in his respect for Saul, the anointed
of God, and in his gracious provision for the one re-

maining son of Jonathan, who "did eat continually at the king's table."

The dynasty had changed, the new marriage between king and people had been celebrated; but both king and people, far from forgetting the past, were to remember it with respect, to "weep over Saul, who clothed you in scarlet," and to do honor to the remnant of the deposed royal family.

Is it not the bride's failure to respect and honor and serve her father that leads to the collapse of many a marriage? Is it perhaps the knowledge of life, as she has learned it in her father's house, that is the most necessary part of the dowry a young woman brings to the marriage bed? And is it not this knowledge of truth that is scorned by society and rejected by the husband who marries her for everything but?

Today's headlines are the culmination of a marriage between an unfaithful daughter and the ingrate who has taken her away—whether the headlines deal with a conceited monster of a nation brought low or with a conceited pretender of a church made ridiculous.

Marriage has to be. A son has to leave his own mother and father to create a new home of his own; a young woman leaves her family home to give life and reality to the dreams of her lover; but the establishment of a new family, a new dynasty, a new priesthood, is no signal to insult and ignore the values of the old.

The statement of John the Baptist that the axe is laid to the root of the tree, and that a tree which is not fruitful will be cut down and cast into the fire, is no statement predicting the future, no idle commentary on ancient history. It is a declaration of the way things are today. It is an equation in time declaiming the fact that, as fruitless trees are to be deprived of their roots, so rootless trees bear no good fruit.

A declaration of independence, a marriage certificate, or a diploma cum laude is not a license to throw out all the heretofore useful wisdom of the ages and suddenly epitomize the wisdom of eternity oneself. *The only kingdom whose throne lasts forever, the only family which stands, is built upon gratitude and respect for the past.* King David, for all his faults, could not have been called ungrateful.

Ethiopia's royal house claims descent from the union of the Queen of Sheba and King Solomon. For a monarchy to have lasted so long, it might very well have begun so auspiciously. Few events are more tempting to one in the visual or performing arts than the arrival in Jerusalem of the caravan of the Queen of the South. The story may be expanded in all directions—photographically, musically, and of course dramatically. The light and the sound and the general hilarity accompanying the grand entry have probably been exceeded, with the help of Thomas Edison, but the glory of the king, the grandeur of his city and of the queen's gifts, and the wisdom of the queen herself can hardly be overestimated. It takes a very wise woman to recognize true worthiness in a man. It takes an even wiser one to bring such a man the knowledge of what, in himself, is truly worthy.

The whole world of men teaches man that his value lies in what he does; a wise woman rejoices in what he is. If he is to her, *her* husband, and to the children, *their* father, and to the world, a man through whom integrity, honor, and courtesy are sustained, it doesn't matter so much if he is the President of Harvard or the shoemaker paid by the piece. If he has achieved in his person a wholeness of reason and strength and affection, more money and more rank may be useful, but they are certainly not essential, and they may very well be harmful. All of Solomon's glory was not essential—for the Queen of Sheba, at least. Having come to praise Solomon, she couldn't stay forever; she had to go home to rule her own kingdom. Judging from the durability of their temporal thrones, *she* seems to have done a good job.

In spite of all of Solomon's eventual weariness with the wisdom given him and his failure to cherish the teaching he had received, in spite of his tragic inability to say no, Solomon's throne too has lasted— not because of what he did, but because of who he was: the son of David.

It is quite conceivable that if Solomon had recognized the true reason for his greatness—simply that he was the heir of his father David—the "love" story might have ended differently. He might have been worth staying for. It is hard to see much lovable within a man who sees so much to love in himself. It may have been hard for Sheba to go back home, but in this respect her wisdom certainly was a match for his.

Remembered for the glory of his lifetime, Solomon is honored; judged by the heritage left his son— hardly.

With all his wisdom, Solomon forgot to be guided by the principle that the glory was derived from the throne of his father David rather than from the fact that he happened for the moment to sit upon it. David's greater Son never made this mistake.

Glory, in itself, is not to be measured as Solomon's glory: not in the riches of the mines, nor in the strength of the horses, nor in the artistic value of the palace treasures, nor even in the number of queens and concubines. The later heirs of the Son of David who measure their glory in the number of marble castles, the value of bejeweled tiaras, or the headcount of cowed communicants, sit on no eternal thrones. The bishops who measure their power by the size of spires, the productivity of lands, or the allegiance of half-baked, undertaught children of all ages, sit on no enduring stones. Christ may share his glory with the least of those who hear his word, but the human

being who presumes to deserve it, either by birth or
by elected or appointed rank, still has a long way
to go. God is still able to raise up children to Abraham
out of the stones of the wilderness.

And *it is in the children that the glory lies.*

The glory had not yet departed from Solomon
when, as a young man, fresh from the example of
his father David, fresh from the teaching of his
mother Bathsheba, and fresh from the holy wisdom
of the prophet Nathan, he was humble before God,
asking for guidance.

The glory is available to every young servant of
God: to every young man who, as a friend of the
bridegroom, would bring the bride of Jesus Christ,
pure and holy, into the presence of her Master. The
wisdom is available not only through the transcen-
dent grace of the Spirit, but also through the straightforward language of the Word of God and through
the straightforward, exemplary lives of those who live
as his image.

But where the glory of the living Word of God is
rejected for the conceits of men, God is still able to
raise up children to Abraham out of the stones of
the wilderness.

And the mothers of these children—the dust, the
stones of whom they are made—laugh bitterly over
the discomfiture of fathers and priests, of presidents
and kings and judges, who, ever learning, never arrive at the knowledge of truth—even when it is to

be found in their own marriage beds, in their own children's cradles.

Life is not with the priest who says, "We consecrate in the contemporary language or with a revised text or by means of a newly programmed catechism." *Life is with the mothers, married or not, who, generation after generation, bear the genes of truth.*

Solomon, in his grandeur, apparently forgot the teachings of his mother, and the Queen of Sheba knew better than to throw her life away on such a man.

Solomon's kingdom was divided not long after his death; and a divided kingdom, even Solomon's, is neither viable nor secure. Neither is it able to succeed greatly in adventures beyond its borders. The complete loss may have taken place long after the death of Solomon, but the seeds of division were planted by every heathen princess he brought into his harem, by every woman to whom his glitter was more glorious than his godliness. It takes a very strong woman to tell a man, even Solomon, that his appeal is in his inherited grace rather than in his slave-made glory. Solomon needed an Esther at home more than he needed Ashtoreth of the Zidonians.

There is a time in the history of every kingdom, every church, every organization, every government, every school, every family on earth, when it needs an Esther at home more than it needs glory abroad.

It needs a Sheba who will visit, look around, exchange gifts, and leave before she herself is destroyed. It needs a Samaritan woman who, in her loyalty to her ideals, will walk out on five men rather than reduce herself to their level of self-deceit. It needs a Bess Truman.

In such matters it is well to remember that any political or historical references may be regarded as parallels to the need of almost every clergyman who ever lived for a wife to tell him that the feeding of the lambs is best done in small flocks rather than in grandiose hierarchies; that the apostolic succession is more by the gift of the Spirit than by the laying on of hands; and that his own work is as the friend of the bridegroom, whose sole purpose is his service to the bride and groom; to tell him, further, that whatever success he has in the world of men is not necessarily the coin of the realm either of the kingdom of God or of the marriage bed. Faithfulness to one's wife and to one's own children is closer to faithfulness to God than is allegiance to the nearest bishop or church president.

No tree is in greater danger of collapse than that one which, unpruned and unfertilized, spreads a spectacular crown in spite of the weak attachment of its roots.

John's warning that the axe is laid to the root of the tree is not an indication that up until the moment of collapse everything has been in good order. His warning is rather that the time has come when, unless the tree is promptly revitalized at the roots and begins to bear in a great hurry, it will, of its own weight, come crashing down. Those who, in the name of unity, in the name of security, in the name of patriotism, have chosen to call their churches American instead of evangelical, who have chosen to clothe their churches in the structures of neoclassical enlightenment instead of in the forms of theological symbolism, who have chosen to have their churches resound with today's vulgarities instead of the vocabulary of the Bible—these men have chosen to bring down upon themselves the wrath of God. And the wrath, as well, of every true mother and father who, having taken their children to church to learn the living Word of God, discover that they will be taught instead the deadwood of educational psychology.

The glory on Sixteenth Street or on Mount Saint Alban's in Washington is every bit as vulnerable as the glory of Solomon's temple—and the destruction no less effective, unless one is willing to learn that feeding the lambs at home is of greater importance than cataloging the national records in Saint Louis or Minneapolis or New York, or checking out the international tabulations in Geneva or Rome.

Obviously, Isaiah's "haughty daughters of Zion," with their chains and bracelets, with their changeable suits of apparel, with their wimples and crisping pins, with the bravery of their tinkling ornaments about their feet—these we still have with us, and in the highest places, where their examples as social successes can best be seen. And those who abjure the earrings and rings and nose jewels clothe themselves with equal grandeur in unimpeachable quotations from Freud and Jung and John Dewey.

To say that salvation is come this day to an anxious Samaritan woman is not to say that it cannot come to the learned, but it is true that salvation is accepted far more frequently by the outcast and her children in the wilderness than by the sons of the kingdom on their thrones.

The sons of the kingdom, for the most part, are so preoccupied with maintaining their own present glory that they neglect to guard the roots of their past and to cherish the fruit of their future.

In
the
Darkness

On
Dying

Recently returned from combat in Vietnam, a young veteran told his fellow students that the death, in his arms, of a comrade shattered by shrapnel wasn't like in the movies: there were no flashings across the skies, no fanfare of trumpets, not even a moment of respectful silence—only blood and death and the continued shooting.

Even under the beautiful solemnity of the Tomb of the Unknown Soldier, there is still only death, and by the eternal flame on the burial site of a fallen president. There are days when the lines of the Mall, from the Capitol to the Lincoln Memorial and from the Jefferson Memorial to the White House, however unintentionally, form a cross on which the expendable die as surely as on the cross of Calvary.

Auschwitz, Lidice, Coventry, Hamburg, Dresden, Pearl Harbor, Hiroshima, and Nagasaki were names for death during the years when today's young soldiers first saw life. Peace, ever since, has hardly been such that death is easily forgotten: the term *overkill* has had to be invented for our age. Death en masse

is the lesson of the day for nations in which individual death is not regarded seriously.

The word *death* itself is avoided as long as possible,
and a mother who has discovered a dead hamster in
the cage will rush out to buy a replacement before
her child gets home from school. Even the English
versions of the Psalms in common usage today speak
of death as the "numbering" or "measuring" of days.
Seldom does one read an English translation as blunt
as Luther's "Teach us to consider, to realize, that we
must *die*, in order that we become wise."

From this point of view, real wisdom is not to be
expected from the individual who pushes to the
farthest depths of his subconscious the fact that he
too must die. Preoccupied with business or science or
government, he may have the power to send other
men to their deaths in order to preserve the national
interest or his own mode of life; but he will never
have the wisdom to know the true values of life until
he stops bookkeeping, note-taking, and head-counting
long enough to consider that he too must die.

We are told that the fear of the Lord is the beginning of wisdom. Is not our "fear" ultimately our awe
and respect of God, our knowing that in his hands
are the keys to life and to death? Wisdom surely begins with the recognition of the reality of death, for
*few of us are wise enough to choose life unless we are
well aware of the imminence of death*. Luther's translation, however free, is surely consistent with the

rest of the biblical message: *the knowledge of death precedes the longing for life, just as the awareness of blindness precedes the joy of sight.*

Whether we sit at the side of the road in the darkness of our blindness, or whether we grovel in the deadening misery of society all around, our cry can only be the same: "Have mercy on us, O Lord, thou son of David . . . that our eyes may be opened." Teach us to die, insofar as trust in our own strength and wisdom is concerned, that we may place our lives entirely in Thy hand, that we may, in darkness, see; that we may, in the midst of death, live.

The value of his own life is plain to the man who considers his death, who considers that the dust to which he returns is the same as the dust of which he was made. Of itself, his life may be nothing. Yet should he in some way—as parent, teacher, supervisor, or governor—be responsible for the life of another, he cannot say of that *other* life that it is worth nothing. Even if he considers that *he* is dust, rejecting the value God places on *his* life, he dare not treat other men as mere dust.

The price paid by God establishes the real worth of a man: "For God so loved the world that he gave his only begotten Son, that whosoever believeth in him should not perish but have everlasting life." These words, and the words of Jesus to Martha after the death of Lazarus, "I am the resurrection and the life: he that believeth in me, though he were dead, yet shall he live: And whosoever liveth and believeth in me shall never die"—these words describing the eternal value and nature of man are spoken at almost every Christian burial service. The dust returns to dust, but the living spirit returns to God who gave it, and gave it value by redeeming it to be his own.

The bright light, the trumpet fanfare, and the awesome serenity of heaven are seldom apparent to the medic in whose arms a soldier dies, or to the chaplain who comforts him in his last moments; but to the man whose soul has at last left the burden of his perishable body, the wonder of the new life must be a glory not to be compared with any beauty of the earth, let alone with the suffering he has left behind. That one dies miserably, that one dies alone, that one dies, leaving behind saddened friends, in no way lessens the incomparable joy of the spirit returned to its rightful home with God.

To strengthen the faith of his disciples, a few days before his own death would shatter them all, Jesus performed yet one tremendous miracle. To show his little flock that even death could not carry them beyond his control, beyond his caring, Jesus called Lazarus back to earthly life. True, some of the mourners wondered why he who had opened the eyes of the blind had not healed his friend rather than let him die; but Jesus had already explained the why of it to his disciples: "It is for the glory of God."

When Jesus had been informed by messengers
from Bethany that Lazarus was ill, his response had
seemingly been contradictory: "This illness is not
unto death." But Lazarus was in fact sick unto death,
for he most certainly did die; indeed, he had been
dead four days when Jesus took himself to Bethany.
Jesus, however, was discussing not the consequence
of the illness, but its purpose. "This illness is not
unto death; it is for the glory of God, so that the Son
of God may be glorified by means of it."

*Death indeed is the consequence of this illness we
call living.* If my purpose is limited to the care and
welfare of others as moribund as myself, the process
of living is only a deadening weight of circumstance.
If my purpose is to live in harmony, in ever present
affection and forgiveness, with my equally moribund
neighbors, my life is still dust. If my purpose is to
live in harmony with nature, it is to dust I return.

Lazarus, no matter how congenial his life with
his sisters, no matter how hospitable his household,
no matter how gracious his role in the village, was
dead. Furthermore, as Martha noted, his body had
in four days begun to decay. His choice of goodness
rather than evil, his willingness to love and forgive
as he had been loved and forgiven and as his Jewish
faith taught him to do—this way of life was no more
the antidote for death than the miserable manners of
the lowest sinner. No sister, no friend, no neighbor
could deny the truth: Lazarus was dead.

To the parent at the deathbed of a precious child, to the grandchildren and children at the deathbed of a beloved grandfather, to the officer counting the fallen among his men, death is real. Death is the one phenomenon about which all observers must ultimately agree, and every one of us is reminded, in the words of John Donne, that, at the funeral of any man, the bell tolls for me. Insofar as I am able to understand the death of any man, in war, in a holiday accident, or in the quiet of his own bed, I die too.

And when I see before me the dead body, does it take more faith to believe that the soul is also dead? or that the soul lives?

For beginners in faith, death is very real but is to be overcome by trust in a Savior who died in our place. For a somewhat more mature believer, death is less real. *Death is what is observed by the bereaved; not what, at the last, is experienced by the dying.*

Psychological studies have suggested that belief in an afterlife is the normal result of the mind's unwillingness to accept the fact of death. If this were so, belief in life after death would certainly be universal. If such belief were universal, one would expect, with allowances for climatic differences and the occasional natural catastrophe, that civilization based upon faith in life after death would be fairly homogeneous, in degree if not in character, over the whole face of the earth.

The belief in life after death may seem, at least in primitives and young children, to be universal, but the understanding of it is not. It is the verbal expression of faith which distinguishes between the baby's wishful thinking and the adult's sure knowledge of eternal life. If the more mature faith, built upon the Word, were as universal as the childish expectation, the fruits of faith would also be universal.

Death is no stranger to the exiles on earth whose homeland is heaven. Death is no enemy to one whose Savior has demonstrated his power over it in the resurrection of Lazarus and in his own resurrection. Nevertheless, the believer has a life to live here.

To the lonely believer, trusting the grace of God to keep his soul alive in a society where the words of life are as welcome as the plague, today's church is a failure unless it stands beside him as he defies spiritual death. The church which has become so much a part of the local or of the contemporary scene, or of both, that it has lost its universality or its eternal quality—that church fails the believer who starves for life. Where and when times are difficult, oppressive or even threatening, the believer comes to church seeking refuge from the smallness of earthly life. He seeks wholeness. He seeks eternity. Even references in architecture or music to other lands or other centuries expand his heart and carry him beyond the confines of the unbearably present

here and now. The experienced voices of other lands
or other centuries teach today's believer how to live,
how to survive dangers, and how, at last, to die. Above
all, the voice of Jesus himself reaches him, through
the words and lives of his fellow believers of all ages,
as well as through the words of the Bible itself.

Jesus, aware of his own imminent death and
equally aware of the dangers to his followers, did not
spend his last few days discussing or solving the
social and political affairs of Jerusalem. Instead, he
filled the minds of his followers with pictures of the
power and the glory of the Father, with pictures of
the unity of himself and his chosen ones with the
Father, with pictures of eternal value. Facing the
awful days and nights of his passion, Jesus occupied
himself with activities designed to strengthen the
faith of the disciples for the terror to come. Even the
entry of Jesus into Jerusalem on Palm Sunday was
not so much for the benefit of the jubilant crowds as
for the instruction of his own chosen ones.

One who sees his own death drawing close has
little time to solve the problems of people halfway
around the world or even across the city. The im-
pending danger compels him to keep close about him
his successors, those who truly matter, to teach them,
to reassure them, to guard them, to encourage them,
to train them for survival so that, as individual believers, they may also escape the judgment and pass
"from death into life."

The Moment
of Revelation

Those few moments when a dying man is not quite here nor there reveal his truest nature. A man whose whole life has been a broadcast demonstration of the joy of the wedding feast celebrating the union of God and man drinks, on his deathbed, not the cup of repentance and justification, but the toast to the Marriage!

The exile falls to the ground, kisses the earth at the gate of heaven itself, and takes off like an Olympic runner for his goal, the throne of his Father.

At death man sees the Messiah, he sees the Father, he sees his homeland clearly: at death man reveals himself in his response.

Though he comes singly to each dying man, Jesus, in his own death, reveals himself to all mankind. During his last few days and weeks he revealed himself particularly to the little group of believers, who, at least as far as their intentions and desires were concerned, refused to leave him. He had eliminated from serious consideration those who were already offended or shocked or confused by his teaching. He was now ready to show his true nature to the small audience remaining. The time had come to reveal himself to them as being the absolute incarnation of the Father, and his "deathbed" testimony and blessing followed the example of every father they had ever known: Abraham, Isaac, Jacob; Moses, Joshua, David; and their own faithful fathers.

Just as a father reveals himself to his children to be their progenitor, their teacher, their protector and provider, so he reveals himself to be a husband to their mother and a friend to every neighbor in need. An earthly father is at one and the same time a son, a parent, and a brother. He is all of these separate and distinct persons, but he is nonetheless one man, the father.

Jesus had spent several years teaching by words and confirming by deeds the nature of God. God was a king, a father, a householder, a landowner, an employer; the sower of seed, the harvester, and sometimes the seed or even the field itself; a creator and a destroyer. God was at one time a root and a branch, a rose and a fruit. God was a stone, a rock upon which to build. God was the dayspring of light in darkness, the balm of the weary, the counselor of the wise; the desire of all nations and the everlasting father; the stone of stumbling, the rock of offense, and yet the prince of peace. To the little group remaining, the Lord before them was also a whole man: he was the water of life, the living bread from heaven, and the eternal word made flesh; he was the son whom David called *Lord* and, like his father David, the shepherd of Israel.

The first step of creation is the elimination of chaos. In his teaching, Jesus first had to say what he was not. "Truly, truly, I say to you, he who does not enter the sheepfold by the door but climbs in by another way, that man is a thief and a robber; but he who enters by the door is the shepherd of the sheep. . . . They know his voice. A stranger they will not follow, but they will flee from him, for they do not know the voice of strangers."

Jesus' teaching was much like that of the English teacher or art instructor who introduces young children to Shakespeare or to Rembrandt, knowing that only a very few will "catch" the passionate truths involved, and that in any case the deepest meaning will not be grasped until much later. But one does not for this reason hold back.

"Truly, truly, I say to you, *I* am the door of the sheep. . . . I am the good shepherd. . . . My sheep hear my voice, and I know them, and they follow me. . . . My Father, who has given them to me, is greater than all, and no one is able to snatch them out of the Father's hand. I and the Father are one."

Even after the evidence of the next few days, after Jesus brought back to his own little flock their beloved Lazarus, not all the hearers understood. Like little children, they heard the words, they saw the miracles; but it was not until later that they realized the meaning. The truly childlike among the people, understanding Jesus clearly or not, believed. It was the men "come of age" who, understanding him very well, from the day of Lazarus's resurrection on, "took counsel how to put him to death."

This distinction, between understanders who do not believe and believers who understand only later, is as clear-cut today as it was during the last week of the life of our Lord, and men continue to take sides accordingly. "Oranges and lemons, / Say the bells of St. Clement's." Every death knell tolls indeed for me, reminding me that *I live and die* either *in the Name of the Father of our Lord* or *in the name of the father of lies. There is no other way.*

One enters the sheepfold by the door, or one is a thief and a robber. One hears the voice of the shepherd and knows his voice and follows him, or one is assuredly a member of some other flock. One is safely in the hand of the Almighty, known to him by name, or one ignores his protection.

One either believes the word which has been revealed to his firstborn by the Father, or one does not; it is certainly to the firstborn Son, even to the firstborn nation, to whom a Father reveals his truest self.

"He who believes in me, believes not in me but in him who sent me. And he who sees me sees him who sent me."

To
the
End

Of the God in whom I put my trust, it must be said that *he* knows. Nothing less will do.

"Now before the feast of the Passover, when Jesus knew that his hour had come to depart out of this world to the Father, having loved his own who were in the world, he loved them to the end. And during supper, when the devil had already put it into the heart of Judas Iscariot, Simon's son, to betray him, Jesus, knowing that the Father had given all things into his hands, and that he had come from God and was going to God, rose from supper, laid aside his garments, and girded himself with a towel. Then he poured water into a basin, and began to wash the disciples' feet, and to wipe them with the towel with which he was girded."

Jesus, knowing from where he had come and to where he should go, knew also how to live on earth. He knew, as Paul learned after him, how to be abased and how to abound. Knowing his own origin and goal, he knew how to accomplish his work on earth.

Knowing that his hour to depart had come, Jesus was able to love his little flock "to the end." He was able to love his own in the humility of service to them, for a master is the servant of all. He loved even Judas, entrusting to Judas more love than the young man could bear. He loved the others, knowing that they were, in the phrase used so often by that disciple who rested on the very bosom of the Savior, dear children, dear little children, and that as dear children of the Father their hearts sought the Father even when their footsteps faltered. He loved them, showing his tenderness toward Peter, who declared his intent to lay down his life for his Lord; and showing his patience with Philip, who still had not understood that in seeing Jesus he had seen the Father. He loved them in his prescient vision of their fate in the world, and he loved them by giving them once more, in summary, the words of eternal life with which they, comforted by the Spirit, would overcome the world. He loved them, not by leaving them to their own devices, but by wrapping them securely in the confines of a new commandment that would make workable the old: "Love one another as I have loved you."

"Having loved his own who were in the world, he loved them to the end."

My dearest children, you who are to me as a branch is to the vine, you who are to me as the very members of my own body, you who are to me the

issue of my own travail—the days are coming when
these figures and parables will no longer be necessary, when you children will yourselves stand face
to face before the Father, asking what you will and
being given it in my name, "for the Father himself
loves you, because you have loved me and have believed that I came from the Father."

*There is a moment in the life of every believer
when his membership in the kingdom of heaven is
sealed: when every child born, not of the will of the
flesh, but of the will of God, comes to himself.* The
fact that there is still a life to be lived between this
birth of the spirit and the final changing to the
wedding garment of eternity does not allow the believer ever to be plucked or grasped out of the care
of the Father, no matter how awkwardly he stumbles
along the way. Once the covenant is sealed, triple-
sealed by the witness of the Father and of the firstborn Son and of the Spirit of Truth, no weakness of
my own nor any power of another can separate me
from the love of the Father which is in Christ Jesus.

Knowing that his hour is come, knowing where he
comes from and where he is going, and loving his
own, he loves us to the end.

"No King
but Caesar"

In every country there are men who, having paid
dearly for their rank and being reminded, as Pilate
was in the presence of Jesus, of the idealism of their
youth, can only respond sorrowfully, "What is
truth?" Almost as surely as the citizen of heaven is
beyond the reach of hell, the man who has sold his
soul for the sake of his own glory is beyond the touch
of grace. Yet Jesus, knowing all things, loved even
Pilate to the end: "You would have no power over
me unless it had been given you from above; therefore he who delivered me to you has the greater sin."

No exercise of the imagination is as futile as the
game of What If. Jesus knew perfectly well the out-
come of his session with Pontius Pilate—as well as
he knew the result of his confrontations in the palaces
of the high priest and of Herod. His time had come,
and there was no foolishness in Jesus' mind about
delaying or rearranging the action. Yet, knowing all
that was to happen, and knowing "that the Father
had given all things into his hands," Jesus showed
himself clearly to be the master of the situation. The

weakness both of the accusers and of the judge in the presence of an innocent man becomes laughable.

Pilate asks first what the accusation is, and the priests answer that if Jesus were not a malefactor they would surely not have brought him. Having talked with the prisoner, Pilate tells the accusers he finds no crime in him; he will have him scourged and released. Not satisfied with the torture of an innocent, the chief priests and officers cry out, "Crucify him!" Then Pilate, knowing full well that they wait only for his permission to put Jesus to death, says almost casually, "Take him yourselves and crucify him, for I find no crime in him."

To Pilate, it matters little how they rationalize the murder of an innocent man—he is hardly noted for his tenderness; but suddenly, to the priests, the justification becomes as important as the crucifixion itself. Their own consciences seek a delay: "We have a law, and by that law he ought to die, because he made himself the Son of God." (Could anyone *less* than the Son of God have silently endured such cant?) Then, when the conscience of the priest is cleared, the heart of the procurator turns to water, and Jesus has to give Pilate courage.

The playacting reaches its climax in the final question of Pilate and in the final answer of the chief priests:

"Shall I crucify your king?"

"We have no king but Caesar."

No scene in the history of mankind is reenacted more faithfully, from one courtroom to another, than this last scene before the crucifixion. *Nothing is more precious to the tyrant than that his tyranny be according to the law, and, if at all possible, required by law! The law, given for a guide and for a refuge to the weak and helpless, becomes a springboard for the violence of the powerful.* Not only does man justify himself by the law, he defends himself against all possible inroads of reason and love by proclaiming that his sole allegiance is to the law. "We have no king but Caesar."

The story is hardly new. *Every government, every set of church authorities, even every set of parents has to make the same choice: have we or have we not a* self-justifying *law? have we or have we not a King beyond Caesar?*

According to Pilate's last word on the subject, we have such a king. The truth is not that Jesus *said* he was a king. The truth is that he *is* the King. Pilate had found the answer to his question, "What is truth?" One wonders why so few of his successors, on their various judgment seats, sacred or secular, learn from his experience!

History describes the rise and fall of whole nations, of grand empires; but *history is far more the record of shepherds than of sheep.* Sheep can be driven, sheep can be bribed; but sheep can also be wonderfully stubborn. They know the voice of their own shepherd: he calls them by name; they hear his voice; and they follow him. A stranger, Jesus tells us, they will not follow, but they will flee from him, for they do not know or recognize—or trust—his voice.

There have to be hirelings. The shepherd, no matter how truly omnipresent, is not always visibly on hand. Long gaps of time and space, even of economic rank or intellectual standing, separate the sheep from each other and from their leaders. Just as children are, in fact, separated from parents by the fact that children are children, so there is an inescapable gap between sheep and shepherd. The hireling is appointed to serve. His effectiveness, often dependent upon his acceptance by the sheep, varies with his willingness to serve as a deputy; with his willingness to follow the example as well as the orders of his commander; with his willingness to learn the same speech, even the same words and inflections, as the true shepherd of the sheep.

How many hirelings, how many high priests does it take to ruin a nation? How many vacillating governors to ruin a province? How many "successful" fathers or newsworthy mothers to ruin a family? How many national presidents, elected elders, or appointed bishops far removed from the local fold does it take to bring about the collapse of the structure of faith?

Abraham stands yet before the Lord: "Wilt thou

also destroy the righteous with the wicked? Peradventure there be fifty righteous within the city. . . . Shall not the Judge of all the earth do right? . . . Oh let not the Lord be angry, and I will speak yet but this once: Peradventure ten shall be found there. And he said, I will not destroy it for ten's sake."

How many righteous men can save the Sodoms of our day, where the voices of the shepherds no longer resemble the voice that the sheep know? For the sake of how many righteous men will the Lord hold back his wrath? Or for the sake of how tiny a remnant will he utterly destroy the wickedness of the city?

There comes a time in the history of power when the destruction of Sodom, of Jerusalem, of Hitler's Berlin, even of a nation's own capital, is more to be desired by the righteous citizen than the preservation of his own life. *That the eyes of the righteous should see wickedness and live is sometimes harder than to look upon it and die.*

It is not the sheep who have "no king but Caesar."

The Veil
of
the Temple

To their hardened attendants in death the victims of Dachau, of Hiroshima, of Hue still leave their garments. To their unknowing brothers far from the final fires they leave the noonday sun, darkened by the wind-carried clouds of death, smoke, and dust; they leave the shattering reverberations of catastrophe and, for a long time afterwards, the insidious fallout of gradually revealed truth.

The wars of our century, even the civil wars or the internal revolutions, with their massive degradation and destruction of human life, have touched whole races and nations with a phenomenon which the seeming peace of the turn of the century had buried: survival guilt. Whole societies learn again that the bearing of this burden is the cost of self-assertion, of self-defense. The alternatives "red or dead" and "black or white" must be considered in the context of the more basic choice: "victim or survivor." This century's experience of survival has made death by firestorm, whether ignited from within or from without, sometimes more attractive than survival. How can a man live when the veil between the world and the holy of holies of his own conscience has been so violently torn?

Eventually the world does press beyond the holy line of demarcation which guards the soul of every man. This is the death of which Jesus speaks when he tells his friends that unless a seed falls into the ground and dies it bears no fruit. This is the death which Jesus himself overcomes, whereby he is able to give to those who trust in him the strength necessary to overcome the death of their own souls. One who has not borne with Jesus the battle of conscience, who has not gone hand in hand with Jesus through the valley of the shadow of death, remains innocent and arrested, in the shelter of the great curtain separating the realities of life from the holy of holies of the conscience within.

One would like so much to return to the womb of the fathers, to the reasonableness of the law, to the sanctuary of Moses; but even a return to the womb demands rebirth. Rebirth over and over again.

Does man overcome what the Japanese writer of survival literature, Yoko Ota, calls the "shame of the living" purely by confession? by repentance? by amendment of life? by a return to the laws which one knows to be the key to life? by a reformation such as Jung describes, based upon a return to the veriest beginnings of mankind?

To a certain extent, yes, of course. There is no salvation without a return to the humility of one's smallest beginnings. But on the other hand who, by his most sincere repentance, can call the dead back to life? This being impossible, shall we go on living, pretending that the age of fratricide is past and that our current age has nothing more to do with it?

Shall we murder the memories of our brothers as well as their bodies? *Worse, shall we shun the pitiful souls, disfigured in body and burned in heart and mind, who arise from the ashes to remind us daily of our universal guilt?*

Will the "work of mourning," even though it were to supplant all the other work of the world, ever suffice to alleviate the loneliness of man for his brother? Will the oneness learned in common sorrow, even though it were to exist among the whole of mankind alive at any given moment, eliminate the sharp and painful line dividing me from my father?

Rebecca comforted Isaac for the death of his mother Sarah, but, for man who refuses to slay his beloved a second time in the act of forgetting, is there any comfort for the loss of one separate, distinct, precious individual? Is there any comfort for the loss of six million older brothers, for the suffering of untold millions of *survivors*?

" 'They parted my garments among them,/and for my clothing they cast lots.' So," writes John, "the soldiers did this."

Few classifications of men suffer in the general opinion of the population as do soldiers. Evidence of the cruel effect of total military life is only too obvious. Yet anyone who has lived, for even a few years, in the midst of an army community uses the term *soldier* with respect. In few other areas of life are things so "seldom what they seem." In only this area of American life, where so much money is spent for death, does the Supreme Court permit the support, with public funds, of a chaplains' corps. The courage of a justice or of a congressman who would deny to a dying man the comfort of his chaplain's presence would be courage indeed.

No man on earth needs more the prayers of his brothers than the soldier who is either defender of or hangman for his society. Seldom in civilian life have I felt the sense of community experienced with a group of officers and their wives, with or without their chaplains, engaged in prayer for the souls of their men. With this in mind, one must remember that the words of love that Jesus spoke to his mother and to his beloved disciple, John, were heard as well by the officers and men who crucified him. The words of grace are spoken to all men.

Only the most naïve supposes that he is not engaged by the death of another. The death of a baby whose mother was not cared for because the father so quickly came and went; the death of a royal prince shot down in ambush; the death of a neighbor by fire

—each is a death in which I share, a part of the universal sin of mankind of which I am a part. *Because all mankind shares the burden of this sorrow —this knowledge that another has died while I go on living—the words of the grace of God must be given to all men.*

To every woman, bereaved no less by the death of her sister's child than by the death of her own, Jesus gives a new son to teach and to comfort. To every one of his brothers, he gives a new mother for whom to care. Both the loneliness of survival and the guilt of survival—the loneliness of separation and the guilt of living when another has died—both of these sorrows are arrested by the words of Jesus, "Woman, behold, your son! . . . Behold, your mother!"

In the awareness of and in the service to those immediately present and in need, the heart disturbed by the irregularity of grief and of conscience establishes once more its steady beat.

It
Is
Finished

"The Lord possessed me in the beginning of his way, before his works of old. . . . I was set up from everlasting. . . . When there were no depths, I was brought forth. . . . When he prepared the heavens, I was there: when he set a compass upon the face of the depth: When he established the clouds above: when he strengthened the fountains of the deep: When he gave to the sea his decree, that the waters should not pass his commandment: when he appointed the foundations of the earth: Then I was by him, as one brought up with him: and I was daily his delight, rejoicing always before him; Rejoicing in the habitable part of his earth; and my delights were with the sons of men. . . . Come, eat of my bread, and drink of the wine which I have mingled. . . . For by me thy days shall be multiplied, and the years of thy life shall be increased."

The bread and wine which we eat are indeed the flesh and blood of the Son of God, who was with him as one brought up with him from the beginning. The words of divine wisdom which we exchange are indeed the Spirit of God, his daily delight. He has given us his body to eat, his blood to drink, and his words to speak. He has given us his own nature, his own spirit, that, singing the words of eternal life, we too may be finished with the words of death.

Eternal life has its whole being in the wisdom of Jesus Christ, who knowing all things offered us the one last evidence of his union with man—"I thirst" —and then the surest evidence of his absolute divinity—"It is finished"; it is complete.

Of the physical existence one speaks in the past, present, or future tense; but the present tense of God is the whole beginning and the whole ending, the alpha and the omega, the presence of every moment of life and the complete fulfillment of all of life, the awareness of every aspect of life and the proper alignment of all properties within the whole.

The circle of eternal life is closed: "It is finished." There may be other worlds, other existences, other realities, but for the believer, the pronouncement of the incarnate wisdom of the eternal and infinite God is enough: It is fulfilled.

Complete fulfillment of life is to be seen not only in the life, death, and resurrection of Jesus, but also in the nature of the Father himself.

What father does not give himself for his children? What father does not give his wisest concern, his physical effort, his deepest feelings, for all of his family? What father does not expect of his firstborn son full allegiance to the name of the father, and at the same time exemplary grace and generosity toward the younger children in the family, toward the mother, and toward even the servants of the household? Finally, what father does not share with such a dearly loved son his full glory, his most delighted approval?

What father is not prepared, if necessary, to discipline, to humble, to alienate, or even to sacrifice— to risk losing the love of—his firstborn, that the others might have life?

Whoever experiences the sacrifice of the firstborn, the loss of communion with the firstborn, or even the ingratitude of the firstborn, is in good company. Abraham, Isaac, and Jacob did no less. It was not for his firstborn, but surely for the son who was first in the eyes of all the people as well as beloved of his father, for whom David lamented in vain anguish: "O my son Absalom, my son, my son Absalom! would God I had died for thee, O Absalom, my son, my son!" Every child was precious to him, even the little one born first to Bathsheba, so that he did not cease to pray for the life of the baby so long as the grace of God might spare it.

It is the nature of the Father to be true to himself, whatever it costs him; to be righteous and to be certain. Therefore Jesus, knowing all things, as one having been with the Father from the beginning, as one brought up with him, had faith that the timing of eternity would carry him beyond the death of the flesh into the glory of his Father.

There is yet a further witness to the power of God over death, over the power of alienation and guilt: his presence today in our own lives. It is because Jesus is in the world working still that John writes that the world itself could not contain all the books that would need to be written to tell the many other things which Jesus did. Even the world itself is too small to hold the results of this work, this touching of the hearts of men with the spirit of eternity—just as one's mother's house is too small to hold easily all the families descended from it.

As each family has a common ancestry and is yet diverse in its own nature, so the children of God, reborn in faith, mature to show all the myriad characteristics of the full nature of God himself.

It is through these varying character traits that God calls to us. He gives us birth in individuality. He calls us by a given name. He speaks to us in a particular language or in particular styles or modes of speech. He even behaves toward us as our separate and distinct characters require. For it is the nature of God to be many things in one, to be diverse and exciting and playful, to be creator and created, to be flesh and mind and spirit, though whole. It is his nature to grasp at once all of time in the eternity of one sentence: "It is finished."

Though God be wisdom and God be love, though God be infinite variety and yet infinite unity, he is of necessity—his necessity and ours—one thing above all: God is faithful.

Though our diversity in nature, as children created in the image of the Father, ranges as widely as life and death, God is faithful. Not limited by our inadequacy, by our misunderstanding, even by our fearful little faith, God is faithful: "He cannot deny himself."

The spirit of truth which unites believers of all time and space, which unites the living and the dead in eternal life itself—this spirit is being faithful, being confident that God, who began a good work in our creation, will bring it to completion in his saving love. We who are told to hold fast to our faith without wavering are also assured that God in whom we trust is faithful. We who are told to *be* faithful unto death are assured that God himself, in his firstborn Son, *is* faithful unto death and even beyond death: so that we who believe in him share with him the crown of life.

The Father gives life to those in whom he delights: this is our justification. There is no other purpose in life; nor any other reason for the survival of one in spite of the death of another; nor any other reason for the eternal life given to him who believes.

The Father has given all things into the hands of the Son, and no one, not even death itself, can take from the Good Shepherd those who hear his voice and come to him.

And the very Spirit of the Almighty is this consistency: the fact that the Father and the Son are One, and that by grace all who are called to be the sons of God share their eternal nature.

"For the law of the Spirit of life in Christ Jesus hath made me free from the law of sin and death. . . . For I am persuaded, that neither death, nor life, nor angels, nor principalities, nor powers, nor things present, nor things to come, Nor height, nor depth, nor any other creature, shall be able to separate us from the love of God, which is in Christ Jesus our Lord."

A Parting Word

Real
Images

A man is known by the language he speaks—either the language of his time and place or the language of eternity. It is by his assimilation of the language of God that a citizen of the world is transformed into a member of the kingdom of God. In this direction the change seems sensible, but how necessary is it for the child of God to be knowledgeable about the language and spirit of the world?

One is chosen, even born, according to the spirit of God, to be a member of the kingdom. Though man lives for a time in the world, he is not of the world, either in the sense that he comes from the world or in the sense that he belongs to the world. How necessary is it for him to understand the modus operandi of the world? One may retain a certain innocence, but dare one remain naïve?

Such questions still persist, even after—or especially after—sure confessions of faith. *God* is faithful; he keeps his promise to be with us throughout our earthly life until the very end. But the more the world impinges on our consciousness with more

116

intensive newscasts or more insistent schoolwork or more frequent committee meetings, the harder it is to be sure of one's own faith in God.

Is there a place for being wise as serpents? Is there a time for being foolhardy? Is there a time when or a place where it is right to lose one's life without exacting the lives of ten of the enemy? Or is there a life in which, popular opinion to the contrary, it is still more important to give a drink of cold water to one's own child than to increase one's rank or income via the cocktail circuit? If there are situations in which one's love for God must supersede one's love for parent or child, is there also a situation in which one's love for the child or one's respect for an aged parent matters more than allegiance to worldly powers? If there are moments when quiet patience is required, is there not also a time when an absolute and decisive stand must be taken? when a choice must be made—against as well as for?

Answers to such questions are indicated by Christ in his commission to the Twelve. His language sounds very unlike his usual words of comfort or encouragement or instruction; but at this moment Christ is not telling stories. He is sending his whole troop into battle. Under such circumstances the only suitable comfort or encouragement is the truth: "I send you forth as sheep in the midst of wolves."

Under ordinary peaceful conditions, we expect to trust each other. We expect to be in agreement with each other. We assume a great deal, and because of the quiet nature of the times we are not proved wrong —unless it is our commission to carry an unpopular message or to request an unwilling service! Then our expectations and assumptions are tried, weighed in the balance, and often found wanting.

During periods of testing, our faith, which dulls in the everydayness of normal life, finds again its strength. Then the promised Spirit of the Father himself speaks through us. Then, in us, the Spirit and the Word give life. Man becomes truly the redeemed image of God: an image, inverted and opposite in a world of light; not *Immanuel*, God with man in the incarnation of the Word, but man made one with God.

It is for this transformation, man made whole with God, that Jesus, God made man, prays when he asks the Father, "Sanctify them through thy truth; thy word is truth." Need one ask more?

Particular Words

THE FATHER

The pattern for man, p. 7, Gen. 1:26–27
Of the prodigal son, pp. 16, 18, Luke 15:11–32
The name of God, p. 18, John 17:1–8
Adoption, p. 38, John 5:19–20
The example, p. 45, John 5:19–20
Choosing, p. 62, John 5:18; 6:44–46; 8:15–19, 39, 47

WORDS

Of eternal life, pp. 11, 14, John 6:68
Babel, p. 8, Gen. 11:1–9
And spirit, p. 25, John 6:63
Materialized, p. 26, John 14:20, 23

WISDOM AND LEARNING

By death, p. 85, Ps. 90:12
Beginning of wisdom, p. 85, Ps. 111:10
Ever learning, pp. 38–39, 2 Tim. 3:2, 7
Reason, pp. 53, 55, Isa. 1:16–20
In the beginning, pp. 109–10, Prov. 8:22–31; 9:5, 11

TRUTH AND BELIEVING

Jesus as Truth, p. 16, John 14:6
Choosing, p. 42, John 3:19–21
Believing in Jesus, p. 95, John 12:44, 45
Defining Truth, p. 99, John 18:37, 38

DEPENDABILITY

Last Things

My Lord,
At last, face to face with you,
I too shall fall in adoration;
Though today
The order is to stand!—
Living proof
That, before my own Master, I stand or fall.

My Lord,
At last, face to face with death,
I too shall fall in victory;
Though today
The order is to live:
Daring now
To stand between the world and our children.

My Lord,
Finally, face to face with eternity
I too shall know transfigured space;
Though today
The order is to wear earth:
Yet asking
That love not judge, by today's fragment, the whole.